WIDOWED

A word on gender usage: In passages referring to financial advisor and client in the abstract sense, we have used the masculine and feminine pronouns, respectively, in order to mirror the relationship between the co-authors of the book and reduce confusion to the reader.

Profits from the sale of this book will benefit the Foundation for Financial Planning, a nonprofit organization dedicated to financial planning education, and nonprofit organizations that assist widows in beginning again personally and financially. For more information, visit www.widowed.com.

WIDOWED

Beginning Again
Personally and Financially

———•———

Sharon Trusty and Barry M. Corkern, CFP
with Sally Crisp

August House Publishers, Inc.
L I T T L E   R O C K

Printed in the United States of America

10 9 8 7 6 5 4 3 2 1

LIBRARY OF CONGRESS CATALOGING-IN-PUBLICATION DATA
Trusty, Sharon, 1945–
Widowed : beginning again personally and financially /
Sharon Trusty and Barry M. Corkern ; with Sally Crisp.
p. cm.
ISBN 0–87483–558–5 (alk. paper)
1. Widows—United States Life skills guides.
2. Widows—United States Finance, Personal.
I. Corkern, Barry M., 1950—
II. Crisp, Sally, 1946—
III. Title.
HQ1058.5.U5T78 1999
305.48'9654—DC21   99-32338

Executive editor: Liz Parkhurst
Project editor: Joy Freeman
Book and cover design: Joy Freeman

AUGUST HOUSE, INC.   PUBLISHERS   LITTLE ROCK

In memory of

John Thomas Trusty
November 11, 1944 – July 23, 1994

The most I ever did for you,
was outlive you... but that is much.
—Edna St. Vincent Millay

Carroll F. Plumlee
December 21, 1929 – October 22, 1983

One can never pay in gratitude;
one can only pay in kind somewhere else in life.
—Anne Morrow Lindbergh

*"For I know the plans I have for you," says the Lord.
"They are plans for good and not for evil,
to give you a future and a hope."*
—Jeremiah 29:11

Contents

Acknowledgements 9

Introduction 13

Loss – Sharon
- The day he died 19
- We didn't want to be apart 31
- If this isn't a rainy day, what is? 33
- I can't start dealing with this yet;
  I have to bury him first 39
- "Daddy, they're playing our song" 47
- I wanted everything in my life back
  just like it had been 51
- Sometimes you just have to go ahead and do it 57
- Loneliness is no longer being the most
  important person in the world to someone 61
- A widow has twice the work with half the staff 65
- I realized everything seemed unfamiliar 69
- "Sharon, honey, I don't think you are
  where you think you are" 73
- You can't buy bread with a piece of steel 77
- I had to find someone who didn't
  see me as just "John Trusty's widow" 81
- You don't have to have a lot of money
  to learn or to plan 83

Coming out of Confusion – Barry

- "What do I do now?" 87
- The only thing that absolutely has to be done 95
- Somebody's got to have a foot on dry land 99
- If you don't have confidence in the person,
  pick up your purse and walk out the door 103
- Fear is the absence of information 107
- Her grief was made harder 111
- You walk in and see a nice foyer...
  and you may be intimidated 119
- The highest standards of conduct 125
- The financial consultant should be a
  relationship manager 131
- The ability to listen is the key 135
- "With all thy getting, get understanding" 141
- You begin to rely on someone again 147

Beginning Again – Sharon

- I had been floating from distraction
  to distraction 153
- I was about to experience the healing
  of my thought life 155
- It's like a slow rain 161
- It's hard to date when you're fifty 165
- I was beginning to see how
  a person might love again 169
- "Are you sure you want to heal?
  Do you really want to move forward?" 173
- "Did you think you'd live to be ninety
  and never have a flat tire?" 177

Epilogue – Barry

- Finding financial freedom 183

Additional Resources 187

Appendices

- Social Security 189
- Debt 191

Acknowledgements

I am indebted to those special people who have been my support system for the past four years, including members of my family, friends, church, and my community, whose constant encouragement has helped me navigate. Thank you for all the hugs and affectionate pats on the back that every widow needs.

Thank you, first, to my incredible family—Bruce, Katherine, Emily, and Rebecca Doberstein; Scot, Jonna, and John Thomas Patterson; Chuck and Jessica Zachary; and my wonderful father, Frank Alexander Steffy—for being so patient and supportive while I was writing this book. I love you all so much.

I owe special thanks to my wise and steadfast friend Jim Burnett, who has brought music to my life. I am grateful to John Lee Philpot for his suggestions and ideas, and for helping me to "stop quitting." A special thanks to Jean Speegel and Jon Lundquist for allowing me to share their professional wisdom with you.

My eternal gratitude goes to Barry Corkern. His input into my decisions is as vital as his input into this book. I owe Barry far more than he knows or will even admit. As much as anyone, he is responsible for whatever emotional stability I have today. More than anyone, he has helped me understand financial matters and enabled me to progress toward total capability. He is a skilled and accomplished professional who has become a champion, not only for me but for many widows.

I extend deep appreciation to our publisher, Ted Parkhurst, for accepting this book for publication, and his enthusiasm in doing so. Thank you, Ted, and thank you, Liz, for your editing skills and for making this project a pleasure.

One of the best things to result from this book is my friendship with Ted, Liz, Barry, Sally, Huey, and their families. I'd like to express my humble gratitude to Sally and Huey Crisp for believing in me. You had more faith in my ability to write than I had in myself, and you always made what I did better. And, thank you, Sally, for so generously displaying your love of this project and making me feel privileged for being able to give to others.

And thanks to you, the reader. Without you, there was no reason to write this book. You are in my mind and heart.

Finally, if this book ministers to you, or if you receive some spiritual or other comfort, encouragement, and knowledge, this is proof that God can use anybody for His purposes. Any credit belongs to the Higher Being who helped me as I lived this experience.

— Sharon Trusty

M y professional experiences working with widows have generated many concerns about their plight. But beyond my clients, I was surprised at the amount of interest in this subject expressed by so many. My thanks and gratitude go out to many friends who have helped me with self-doubt. They gave me confidence that what I think, hear, and see about working with widows matters and can be helpful to many.

Although I am passionate about my work as a financial consultant, the idea of writing a book did not come easily to me. Ted Parkhurst and I have been friends for years. I have a great deal of respect and admiration for him as a person and a businessman. Consequently, his opinion as a book publisher was most significant. After submitting an outline of a speech I gave at church, I asked for his thoughts on writing this book. His simple response of "I think you should write this book" was exactly what I needed to get started.

Del Medlin, my pastor, helped me identify my mission. He reinforced the importance of helping widows and pointed out that someone need-ed to address the issues that widows face. What he has given me helps me to give in return. Joe Park, Jr. is president of a small-town bank. He and I see the world much the same way. Without his support and encouragement, this book could not have been written. My thanks, also, to Edgar J. Tyler, a knowledgeable, caring tax and estate attorney, who helped me avoid technical errors.

I would like to express my deep appreciation to Sally and Huey Crisp for their work in writing this book. Their experience and expertise were immensely helpful. Sharon and I relied on their technical knowledge countless times. Their work saved many, many hours, which permitted me to continue my practice while completing this project. They gave us constant encouragement, telling us that we were on track, telling us that this work needed to be done. They have given me insight and confi-dence in my work and my desire to help others.

Looking back over the past fourteen months, I believe it was Divine Providence that connected Sharon Trusty's life with mine. When I met her, little did I know she would give me the courage and conviction to write a book. Once we decided to go forward, she was always there with her support and encouragement. Writing a book is no small task in terms of time and emotion. Any time I expressed doubt or frustration, her commitment kept me on course. Her courage to speak so freely and frankly about her experiences (many parts of this book were very difficult for her) gave me courage. Her dedication to help other widows made me more dedicated. She is a good example of the "givers" in this world. It is very easy to respect the great person she is. I would never have tackled this project without her.

My thanks to my wife, Jan, and my daughter, Lauren. They struggle daily with the idiosyncrasies of living with a "workaholic." Yet they patiently accommodated my need to take on another project, knowing it would take time away from my being a husband and dad. I appreciate their support for the demands of writing this book and for the future demands that will result from it. Their love, support, and pride carried me through many hours of work. Jan, I thank you for being a wonderful mother, for being a great "decision partner," and, most of all, for giving me the courage to let Christ have my life.

Most of all, I wish to thank my clients. If it had not been for all the people I have worked with over the years, I would have little, if anything. My clients have fulfilled my dream of having my own financial consulting business. My passion for helping those in need is fed every day of my life. Thanks for the opportunity.

— Barry Corkern

I am grateful to all who have collaborated on *Widowed.* I am especially grateful to Ted and Liz Parkhurst for inviting me to be a part of this project. I'm grateful to many people for their help and support, especially my friends Virginia Scott and Emily Sudderth, for their thoughtful reading of the manuscript, and to my colleagues Allison Holland, Cheryl Harris, Larry Henthorn, Vicki McCollum, and Jim Frazer for their help and support.

I am grateful every day for the encouragement of my daughters, Mitchell Crisp Patterson and Molly Crisp, and of my mother, Lucille Chandler Bryson. I am grateful, most of all, to my main collaborators: my precious husband, Huey Crisp, without whose help, support, and understanding I could not, would not attempt a project like this one; and, most important, to Sharon Trusty and Barry Corkern, who are the heart of this project. I know this has been a labor of love for you; I appreciate so very much the opportunity to be a part of it.

— Sally Crisp

Introduction

Every book is a collaboration. Writer, editor, artists come together to produce what you select from the shelf or catalog. It's not at all unusual to see the names of two, three, even four writers on the cover of a book—a bringing together of backgrounds and talents, of experiences and expertise. This book has emerged through just such a collaboration, one that has involved a special sort of teamwork and synergy, and an extraordinary bond of commitment.

Widowed is the result of the teamwork between a woman suddenly widowed—and, truthfully, lost—and the advisor who helped her regain her life. It is intended to offer her experiences, to share his expertise, to encourage and help others.

———

"I used to have an attitude about change," Sharon Trusty writes. "Everything good was permanent. The things I wanted to last would last. Anything else was an interruption." What Sharon has experienced—what many women, and men, have experienced or will experience—was much more than an interruption.

Sharon and John Trusty were living the American dream. They lived in a picturesque college town in the Ozark Mountains of west-central Arkansas. John was a successful businessman and civic leader. Sharon had been a stay-at-home mom for a number of years; she was active in her church and community. They had a beautiful home, the warmth and comfort of their daughters and their sons-in-law, two young granddaughters, extended family, and many, many friends in and beyond the community. They had many hopes and plans for their future.

On that July day when her husband John died of a heart attack at forty-eight, the life Sharon knew changed suddenly and drastically. Sharon lost the husband whom she loved, whom she counted on. She also lost a measure of her identity and, as she describes it, her sense of familiarity with the people, and things, and processes in her life. And when she lost John, she gained the job of coming to grips with her financial circumstances. She entered a period of profound confusion.

"A widow always needs a good, objective advisor — a decision partner," Barry writes. When Sharon sought help from him, Barry had had a number of years' experience as a financial consultant; he had counseled many clients, among them a number of widows. Barry recalls the first widow he met — a woman to whom he delivered an insurance benefit check as a young man. He recalls the first widow whom he served in his practice as an independent financial consultant. After close to twenty years, he still counts her among his clients. When Sharon came to meet with him, he listened, and they began to consider her circumstances and the decisions she faced.

Soon after they began, Barry asked Sharon if she would give him some suggestions on a church presentation he was to present. The working title was "How to Be a Good Widow: Making Proper Financial Decisions." She offered some suggestions. The presentation went well, and Barry reported back to Sharon that some people from his audience had told him, "A book like this could be very helpful." Sharon recalls that she smiled and said, "People have said the same thing to me." From this beginning the idea for this book grew.

Barry knew the risk in undertaking such a project with a client — but Sharon assured him she could keep the project separate from their work on finances. Sharon had looked in vain for a book to help her understand her financial matters, indeed to understand her would-be advisors. Barry felt that a book introducing the concept of an objective advisor as a trusted decision partner could be helpful to widows and advisors alike. The idea simmered. Over coffee, they discussed their mutual sense of calling about writing the book. It was the beginning of their extraordinary synergy, extraordinary commitment.

In Part I, Sharon shares the story of her loss and her descent into confusion. In Part II, Barry offers information — a roadmap leading out of confusion. Drawing on Sharon's experience and his experiences with other widows, he introduces the decision partner concept and offers ways of understanding, through which widows can come to make their own decisions, to act in their own best interests. In Part III, Sharon tells of beginning again.

Who should read *Widowed?*

First of all, widows, or those who are going to be. Many woman will be widows, a fact about which most have a dangerous attitude: *it won't happen if we just don't think about it.*

Second, widowers. Almost every step of a widow's journey can be the same for a widower.

Moreover, family members and friends of someone who has been recently widowed should find insight here and be aided in their efforts to be helpful.

Finally, all those who advise widows and widowers, including attorneys, accountants, stockbrokers, financial consultants, and others in the financial professions. For those who work with widows, this book is a window into their lives, one that illuminates what it is like to lose your spouse, your trusted decision partner.

———•◦•———

Widowed offers two voices in one book: it teaches about finances, but it is as much about healing as about finances. In fact, Sharon knows that understanding her finances has helped her heal: "That these two go together is an important message to women who may be reluctant to step out and take action. If I hadn't found help to address my financial matters, I don't know if I ever would have regained confidence in myself." Barry believes the decision partner concept can give advisors a better understanding of widows, can help widows and their advisors know how to work together.

I am glad and grateful I was invited to be a part of this collaboration. It has been my privilege to know and work with Sharon Trusty and Barry Corkern in writing this book. I hope — I trust — you will feel it's been your privilege to know them through these pages.

Speaking for the three of us — Sharon, Barry, and myself — we wish each one of you courage and hope as you plan for your future.

— Sally Chandler Crisp
Little Rock, Arkansas

Loss

———•———

Sharon:
*I wanted everything in my life
back just like it had been.*

The day he died

I t was very warm that Saturday morning. As I walked across my yard, I was thinking of all the projects John and I had going. We had started an addition to our home; our youngest daughter, Jessica, was getting married in exactly two weeks; we were to leave for Japan two days after the wedding; and John and his partner were in the middle of some major changes in their business.

John was very involved in politics, and that morning he was supposed to go to the Johnson County Peach Festival in Clarksville. Earlier in the week I had asked him not to attend any more political events until after Jessica's wedding. I thought he should be helping with the wedding preparations.

When he got up that morning, he was willing to stay home. But I said, "No, that's OK; go ahead." John had made arrangements to meet Miss Ada Mills — she is in her eighties, and John loved her dearly — at the festival, and I hated for him to disappoint her. But he stayed home.

John's favorite restaurant was Cagle's Mill at the Holiday Inn in Russellville. He ate there morning, noon, and night when he could — and they pampered him. They would always bring out an extra bowl of fried okra, pinto beans, or something he liked. That morning, he went to the Holiday Inn for breakfast and then came home.

We decided to do some yard work before it got too hot. Our oldest daughter, Katherine, had brought her two little girls, Emily and Rebecca, over to swim. Jessica joined them in the pool. We ordered pizza, and as I walked across the yard toward the pool, I said a prayer of thanksgiving: "Thank you, Lord, that we are both healthy. I know You wouldn't take either one of us in the middle of all of this because if You did, the other one wouldn't survive."

I was really getting hot. I was trimming the forsythia at the end of the pool. I put down my clippers, and I jumped in the pool. I said to John, "Come and get in the pool with us and cool off."

But he said, "I'm almost finished."

In a little while, Katherine said, "Mom, is there something wrong with Dad?" She had a puzzled expression on her face.

I looked around the yard where he had been working. "Where is he?"

She frowned. "He's over there on that pile of lumber."

I saw him about twenty feet away, lying on lumber stacked in the yard by our contractor. I thought he was just resting in the shade. I called out to him, mostly to reassure Katherine: "John, are you OK?"

"Yeah," he said, "I'm just a little sick to my stomach."

Uh oh, I thought. *He's having a heat stroke.* "Maybe you'd better jump in the pool and cool off," I called.

Slowly he got to his feet. "No, I think I'll go in and lie down."

That got my attention. He would *never* lie down in the middle of the day.

Just then, the pizza we had ordered arrived. John didn't like anyone to hover, and I knew that if I went in and asked him how he was, he would get upset with me. So I told the kids, "I'm going to go check on your dad and pretend I'm bringing him some pizza."

At first, I couldn't find him. When I did, he was on his hands and knees in the bathroom of our master bedroom, leaning over the commode like he was throwing up. His eyes were rolling back in his head. I said, "You're having a heat stroke; we are going to the hospital."

"No," he protested, "just give me a minute and I'll be all right."

Thoughts began racing through my mind. John was always a "take-charge" person, but I could see he needed me to be in charge now. I thought to myself, *If I call 911, he will be so upset with me he'll have a heart attack. If I look overly concerned, he'll be frightened.* I remained calm, coaxing him to allow me to drive him to the hospital.

I knew *he* was concerned when he let me put some blankets

on the floor and pour cool water over him. Then he allowed me
to help him to the shower, and I turned the spray on him. *If he
passes out*, I thought, *I'm calling 911*.

Our neighbor, Johnny Cornwell, is a pharmacist. John said,
"Run next door and see if Johnny's home. Maybe he'll have
something." I ran next door and was relieved Johnny was home.
"Johnny, could you come over? I think John may be having a heat
stroke."

On my way back to the bedroom, I grabbed the portable
phone, not knowing what I would find when I got there. John was
still sitting on the floor of the shower with the water running. His
eyes continued to roll back as though he was about to pass out.
It was obvious he was in some kind of distress. Johnny checked
his pupils and took his pulse.

"Are you having any pain in your chest?"

"No, I just have this tunnel vision."

"Is your arm or shoulder tingling?"

"No. I'm just a little short-winded, and I keep feeling real nau-
seous."

"I need to run home and get something," Johnny said. "I'll be
right back." While he was gone, I tried once again to get John to
go to the hospital. But he insisted, "I'll be all right."

Johnny came back with his stethoscope. He listened to John's
heartbeat and said, "You know, John, I think it's a heat stroke and
you're going to be OK, but you need to go to the hospital and let
them check it out in case it's not. Let them pump some fluids into
you." When Johnny suggested it, that made it OK. I felt tremendous relief because I was beginning to think time was of the
essence.

I called to the girls, who were still in the pool. Katherine came
inside while Jessica stayed out with Emily and Rebecca. Not
wanting to further alarm them, I simply said, "Katherine, we are
going to the hospital to have your dad checked out." I went to get
the car out of the garage while she walked John out to the car. I
knew she was frightened. She stood watching while we drove out
of sight. John was still in his swim trunks and baseball cap. He
had grabbed a shirt on his way to the car. I was still wearing my
swimsuit and big white cover-up.

On the way, John started leaning forward in the front seat, like he was trying to hurry. That concerned me, and I drove faster. When I pulled into the emergency entrance, he said, "You can't park here." I said, "Yes, I can until I get you inside."

I took him into the emergency room. I told the admissions clerk, "I think my husband is having a heat stroke."

Before I had time to explain further, a door opened and several nurses came out. One said, "Come on in." They took him back immediately, which was strange to me. There were other patients in the waiting room, and no one even asked for paperwork — that's how quickly the ER personnel responded. Later, I found out that when Johnny had come to the house with his stethoscope, he couldn't get a heartbeat on John. He was torn between riding with us to the hospital or going home to call ahead and alert them. He decided it was more important to call the hospital. He told them John was having some heart problems — that he couldn't get a heartbeat — and to get the machines and the paddles ready. That's why they took him in so quickly.

They immediately opened the door to the waiting room and said, "Come in, Mrs. Trusty." Relieved he was in good hands, I ran to park the car, which probably took less than two minutes. When I returned, they already had him in a room; he was lying on a table, and they were scurrying around pulling carts, machines, equipment.

John still had his baseball cap on.

"Do you want me to take your hat?" I asked him.

"No." I have tried to remember what the last thing he ever said to me was: I think that was it: "no." I don't think he ever said anything else to me.

At the time, I thought that was strange because John Trusty would never have worn a hat indoors under normal circumstances.

One of the nurses said, "Mr. Trusty, we're going to hook you up to a heart monitor," and began explaining the procedure. *That's strange*, I thought. *He is having a heat stroke; why are they hooking him up to a heart monitor?*

Suddenly a nurse said, "He's in V-fib!" Then she yelled, "Marilyn, get in here! Marilyn, get in here!" Then the room filled with emergency personnel. A nurse asked me to leave, then turned back to the table where John was. He was not unconscious — he just looked around with a wild expression — and even attempted to get up. I didn't leave; I wanted to know what was happening, but I couldn't get near him. He was surrounded by people and equipment. Between openings of arms, cords, and white coats, I watched as they used the paddles to shock him.

"You *have* to leave!" a nurse said, this time more insistent. I didn't want to distract anyone. I wanted every one of them to take care of my husband, so I left.

As I stepped into the hall, I understood. His heart had stopped.

I went into shock. It was like sticking your finger into a light socket while having cold, icy water poured down your spine. It was a physical feeling that I would experience many times.

Then I thought, *Oh, the heat stroke has stressed his heart; they will get it beating properly, then give him some fluids. But he may have to spend the night.*

In a little while the nurse came out. She was so good with me. "Mrs. Trusty, we got his heart going again; you can go in now."

"Is he having a heat stroke?" I asked.

"He's real sick."

But I insisted. "Well, he's going to be all right?"

"Mrs. Trusty, he is just real sick."

So I went in. He sat up, looked at me, opened his mouth to say something to me — and started fibrillating again. He didn't pass out. Again, they shocked him and made me leave the room. Again, I went through those feelings of shock. Electric, cold, up and down my spinal column.

Over the next few hours, this would happen about thirty times. Each time a nurse would come out to tell me what was going on. Each time the report was the same. "Mrs. Trusty, he's real sick."

"Is he going to live?" I finally asked.

"We're trying to keep him alive."

"Is he having a heart attack?"

She confirmed it: "Yes, he's having a major heart attack."

The doctor on call was a family practitioner from Millard-Henry Clinic. I asked the nurse, "If he's having a heart attack, why isn't Dr. Soto here?" Dr. Soto was a cardiologist in Russellville. John and

I had gone to school with his wife, Katherine, although we had never used him professionally. There had been no heart problems until now.

The nurse explained the policy: the doctor on call checks the patient and decides what specialist is needed.

"What if I request that Dr. Soto be called?" I asked.

"You can do that."

"Then get him here."

In just a little while, Dr. Soto arrived. Several times they came out and told me I could go in. Each time John would look at me and try to speak, but he never could tell me what he wanted to say because he would go into V-fib. I began to wonder if my being there was stressing him further. He knew what was ahead for me. I still wonder what was going on in his mind because there was something he tried to tell me every time I went in.

It took me months, but I went back and talked to the nurses who were there that day and asked them about what had happened. I wanted to talk with the people who had helped him, and I wanted to know what he had been trying to say to me.

They said the first time they shocked him, he got off the table, stood up, and said, "Thanks guys, I needed that." The second time he did the same thing and said, "I'm going home."

"No, you're pretty sick, Mr. Trusty; you're going to have to hang around."

"Am I having a heart attack?"

They told him, "Yes, you are."

"Umm. I guess I should have listened to my wife."

They came out and asked me if there wasn't somebody I could call, but I shook my head. The only people I wanted were my children, but I thought, *I can't call them and tell them their father's heart has stopped.*

I'm not sure what I was thinking; I suppose I thought he was going to be OK and the girls would never have to know. Maybe there was a possibility they would never have to go through what was happening. Maybe I could spare them.

Finally, they insisted. "Mrs Trusty," they said, "You need someone with you."

I didn't ask why. I was afraid to. The only person I knew to call was Johnny. I couldn't remember his phone number, but someone got him on the phone for me. He was waiting for my call.

"Johnny, can you tell the girls to come to the hospital? John's heart has stopped—but don't tell them that."

"Well, what do you want me to tell them?" he asked.

"Well, they got it going again; so don't tell them that his heart stopped."

"What do you want me to tell them?"

"Just tell them that they need to come down here. I don't want them to be scared and have a wreck."

He said, "I'll tell them whatever you want me to tell them, but what do you want me to tell them?"

"I don't care what you tell them," I yelled, "Just get them here!"

Even before he died, the decisions started: *Mrs. Trusty, is there somebody you can call?* When do you call them? What do you say?

When Katherine and Jessica walked in, they knew.

I said, "He's real sick."

Jessica looked at me. "Mama, Daddy's not going to die, is he?"

"Honey, I don't know, but it's really bad." I didn't want to tell them, but I knew the answer. I felt God was preparing me for it by allowing me to think it was going to happen. John and I had been married for over thirty years, and it was on one level unthinkable that he was going to die. But I kind of knew, and this made me believe God was preparing me. I tried to convey that to the girls without saying, *He's probably not going to make it*. I just said, "It's really bad. His heart has stopped, and they have had to use the paddles to get it going again."

I don't know how long it took for us to realize we hadn't called Jonna, our middle daughter, who lived in Fort Smith, about eighty miles from Russellville. When Katherine asked, "Mom, don't you think we should call Jonna?" I realized I hadn't even thought about it.

Thank goodness she and her husband, Scot, were home. This was unusual for a Saturday. Jonna was sleeping, and Scot answered the phone—also unusual. He was there for Jonna, something else I've been thankful for. Katherine explained the situation to him, and they were on their way.

In a little while, Katherine asked me, "Mom, don't you think we should call our minister?"

"No, " I said, "because I don't want a lot of people here. I need to pray, and I don't want a bunch of people here asking questions and trying to talk to me."

Katherine persuaded me. "Let's just call Chuck and tell him to have everybody else pray for Daddy." So she called our minister and as word spread, people started drifting in. Most of those who came at first were members of the hospital staff. John and I had many friends in the medical community, and as word spread throughout the hospital, people began to arrive.

Beverly Smith, once widowed herself, came in with tears streaming down her face. "What do I do?" I asked her. She hugged me and replied, "I don't know."

Several physicians happened by. Though they didn't have to, both Dr. Crouch and Dr. Beavers stayed the whole time. I've never forgotten that. Jessica's fiancé, Robert, arrived. I was glad he was there for her.

As more and more people arrived, the small waiting area became congested. Emergency room personnel led us to a small room close to where they were working on John. They kept asking, "Would you like to go in now?"

We would go in, and the same thing would happen. Over and over again. He would sit up, try to speak to us, and his heart would stop again. I remember thinking, *They're letting us spend as much time with him as possible. They think he's going to die.* I found out later I was right. I just wanted them to fix him and *then* come and let me see him.

It was beginning to upset me, and it must have showed. They said, "You don't have to go in." I said, "Oh, yes I do."

How could I not? At the time, he was still awake—they had not yet intubated him. We told him we loved him. We would hold his hand until they would push us away so they could use the paddles.

The nurse later told me that he was able to talk to them. They would tell him, "Tell us when you are about to go out, Mr. Trusty."

And he would tell them. He kept asking if his girls were there. They said, "Yes, they are just outside."

"All of them?"

"Yes, both of them are here," they answered.

"No, there's another one."

Several times he asked her, "Is there someone with my wife?"

I asked her, "Was he afraid?"

She said, "Yes, he was. He asked me to hold his hand."

I'm sorry I wasn't the one. If I have any regrets, it's that I didn't hold him. When we were home in the bathroom, I wanted to hold him. When he was there, I wanted to hold him.

They came out and told us they thought he was stable enough to move to the Coronary Intensive Care Unit, but they needed to intubate him. I think this was when his condition worsened to the point that he lost consciousness. By this time, several friends who were physicians were there; they moved in and out, checking on him and keeping us informed.

When we stepped off the elevator on the Intensive Care floor, I was shocked. The waiting room was totally full of people — family, friends, church members. I remember thinking, *Where did they come from? How did they find out so quickly?*

All I wanted was to be with my girls. I didn't want anybody taking my mind away from my prayers, or from my girls. But everyone was so kind. It was as though they sensed my needs. They very quietly sat with me, coming over occasionally to hug or pat me.

Dr. Soto came out. "I don't think we are going to be able to save him, but there is one more procedure we can do. I don't think it will work, and it is very expensive."

That was an easy decision. "Do it," I said.

Meanwhile, someone asked, "Would you like for me to call Linda Bewley?" Linda is one of my dearest friends. I needed her. She always knew what needed to be done. When she arrived, she took one look at me and said, "Do you want me to go back to your house and pick up some clothes for you?"

I was still in my bathing suit and cover-up. "Yes, I'm cold."

"What do you want me to bring?"

"I don't know."

"Where's your hair dryer?"

"I don't know." It was the only answer I had.

Linda went to my house and came back and helped me dress. "Don't you think we should call his brothers?" she asked.

"Well, yes."

Decisions. Where can I get their phone numbers?

"Don't we need to call Bill Mitchener? Jim Burnett?"

Jonna arrived. She got off the elevator with her usual spring in her step, saw the waiting room full of people, and semi-collapsed. She knew. She found me and said, "Mom, is he dying?" I said, "They don't think he's going to make it." We told the nurse to go tell John that Jonna was there. Later the nurse told me: "You know, I think he was waiting for all of his girls to get there before he died."

The hallway to the Coronary Intensive Care Unit is long. Dr. Soto was walking toward me; his nurse was with him. *She should stay with John,* I thought. She had never come with him before when he came out to talk to us. I looked at the doctor. He had his hands in his pockets and was looking out the window as he walked toward me. Then I knew. I thought, *Oh no, somebody needs to go get my girls.* I knew what I was going to hear, and I didn't want to hear it twice.

Dr. Soto said, "I'm sorry."

Jonna was unable to comprehend the situation because she had not been there long. "You mean he died?"

Dr. Soto nodded his head and said, "He expired."

Again, she asked, "He's dead?"

There came that same shock feeling again. Cold, electricity, up and down my spine.

We just waited for direction. What are you supposed to do? A nurse asked, "Do you want to see him? Do you want anyone else to see him?" I wanted to see him and so did the girls. I asked his brothers who were there, Donald and Charles, if they wanted to see him. Perry had not arrived yet. I did not want anyone other than immediate family to see him because I don't think he would have wanted them to.

Scot, Jonna, Katherine, Jessica and I went in. He looked so peaceful.

I wanted to hold him, but I didn't because I was afraid it would upset my girls. I wanted to hold him because I felt like that would be a goodbye for me. I never said goodbye; even though I was there, I never told him goodbye. I had told him I loved him, and I had said, "Everything is going to be fine." I didn't want to say, "Don't worry about me" or "Goodbye." I didn't want him to think that I thought he was going to die; so I was very careful about what I said and how I acted. But I wish I had held him.

I don't remember what we talked about. I remember standing there in the ICU, trying to let it soak in that he was gone. Dead. I remember thinking, *So this is what it's like*.

We went to a room the hospital administration had prepared for us so that we could have some privacy. We started trying to figure out who we needed to call. Katherine's husband, Bruce, is a pilot; she began trying to locate him. She called the Delta Family Emergency Number and learned that he had just taken off on a flight from Dallas to Phoenix. She didn't want him to get the message while he was in the air, so she left a call-back number.

"Mrs. Trusty, we need to call a funeral home. Which one do you want to call?" We told the nurse which home to call and she came back and said it would be a while before they could get anyone there to pick him up. I told everyone I wanted to stay until they came for him. I wanted to be with him as long as possible. I didn't want to leave him alone.

We didn't want to be apart

I don't remember the drive back home. Jonna remembers that she drove me, but she can't remember if we were alone or if someone rode with us.

I do remember thinking how strange everything was — earlier John had sat where I was sitting. He would never sit there again. He had been alive. We had driven down this street together and never would again. We had started our life together here; we had been married in Russellville. Neither one of us had known that would be the last time we would ride down Main Street, Russellville, Arkansas, together.

When we got to our street, I was totally unprepared for what I saw. I didn't think anybody would know about his death except the people who had been at the hospital. But you couldn't get in the street. The yard was full; there was no place to park. Jonna tells me I looked at the cars and said, "It's real, Honey, isn't it?"

When we went inside, the house was full of people. I remember seeing Judy Taylor and Jeanette Burgess coming down my hallway with my laundry. Food was being delivered, and the phone was ringing continuously. I am still amazed at how fast the word spread. I was trying to prepare for the onslaught of questions and decisions. I knew we had to think about funeral arrangements. I knew that there would be questions about the wedding. I knew the trip to Japan had to be canceled, and I knew the house project would have to be put on hold. But first I needed to tell everybody that John Trusty had died.

People wanted to talk to me on the phone; they wanted to know if it was true. Everyone found it hard to believe: "Is it true?" "When?" "How?" "Did he suffer?" "Are you OK?" "When is the funeral?"

I couldn't believe anyone would expect us to have any arrangements made scarcely four hours after his death. I wanted them to call the funeral home for that information. I was drained, and I had nothing left to give. Finally, my nephew Tom asked, "Would you like for me to handle the calls?"

"Oh, yes, please."

I was exhausted. I don't know what time it was — seven, maybe eight o'clock. Somebody asked if we wanted medication to help us rest. Under normal circumstances I'm not inclined to do that, but these weren't normal circumstances.

When I got to the bedroom, I realized why my friends had been doing my laundry: the blankets were gone, the shower stall empty. There were no signs of what had happened; the bathroom was clean.

That night was awful, yet, looking back, it was also bittersweet. My three girls wanted to sleep with me. We didn't want to be apart. I think we were all afraid that something else might happen to one of us. Like teenagers at a slumber party, we made beds on the floor of my bedroom so we could sleep together. Scot had a choice of either sleeping with his wife, his mother-in-law, and his two sisters-in-law, or sleeping alone. He chose the couch in the den.

The prescription the doctor had given us said, TAKE TWO. We were all so tired that we thought one would be enough, so we each took one. Scot, who had been raised Christian Scientist and had never even taken an aspirin, took one too.

But none of us could sleep. Katherine, thinking we were asleep, got up and went into the den and started to cry. Scot immediately woke up and cried with her. She took a second pill and came back to the bedroom. Meanwhile, Jessica got up and went to the den to cry and woke Scot up again. Together they cried. Katherine went back to the den, and Jonna decided to get up, thinking I was asleep. Finally I gave up too and went to the den. The rest of us took our second pill and waited to get sleepy. It never happened.

We stayed up and talked all night. We sat there, the five of us, and talked about good things and bad things. We talked about the wedding. Jessica was concerned about what to do. I told her, "Let's just get through the funeral first."

If this isn't a rainy day, what is?

The next morning I was shocked to see on the front page of the paper a color picture of John. The headline read, *Local Business and Civic Leader John Trusty Dies.* Seeing it in print was probably good for me. I didn't cry; I was afraid that if I started to cry, I would never stop. I read it and thought, *Now people won't forget him.*

Later in the day someone drove me to the funeral home. I remember thinking, *Why is everybody going on about their business? John's dead.* I thought everything ought to stop. I have heard others say they felt that way when they lost someone close. But no matter how bad your heart is breaking, the world doesn't stop for your grief.

Earlier in the day, John's accountant had come by. By that time I had already thought about all that I didn't know. Two days earlier, I had been very secure with what I thought I knew.

Some of the things the kids and I talked about the night before raised a lot of questions. I knew John and I had savings. I knew we had a will. I knew we had investments. I knew there were business interests. We were in the beginning stages of the construction on our house. I *didn't* know the balance of that account. I didn't know which materials had been ordered or which were already paid for. Was the business paid for? Were the other assets debt-free?

"Mom, you aren't going to have to sell the house, are you?" Jessica had asked. "Of course not," I said. But I didn't know. She had one more year of nursing school, and she asked, "Am I going to have to quit school?" Of course I said, "No." But I didn't really *know.* I thought I could always sell the house if I had to. I felt I needed to say whatever would make her feel more secure, but I *really didn't know*. At that point I made up my mind. I would use the savings to pay for the wedding if I had to. I would use the savings to get me to the point where I could figure something out. I thought, *If this isn't a rainy day, what is?*

But I was frightened about my long-range future. When I talked to the accountant, I just said, "Am I going to be all right?" He was hesitant, but he gave a sort of qualified yes. I was too numb to ask him to elaborate. I thought, *He's got bad news; he knows something, but he is not going to tell me right now. And that's OK. I don't want to hear it right now. I have to go to the funeral home. I'll hear it later*.

Katherine, Jonna, and Jessica were very concerned for me. They were so strong. I watched them become adults during this time. But I felt that since they had just lost their father — with whom they all were uncommonly close; all three had been "daddy's girls" — I didn't want them to feel insecure. I didn't want them to think their father's death was going to ruin everybody's life forever, even though *I* thought so. I didn't want them to see my pain. They had their own pain without worrying about me.

I can't imagine attempting to make funeral arrangements for your spouse if you've never before been involved in planning a funeral. It helped that I had. Who will conduct the services? Where you are going to hold them? Who will provide the music? What songs will be sung? Who will be pallbearers? You have to decide on the order of the service. You have to take into account how long it will take the family members to get there.

We went to the funeral home, where we faced another decision: what was he going to be buried in? Though John would spend his last dime on the children and me, he would wear shoes with holes in them! Throughout our marriage, we had conducted an ongoing " argument" about the way he dressed. I would buy him clothes, but he wouldn't wear them. He had a sports jacket that was so old I threw it away — and he went to the garbage and retrieved it! Next I put it in the washer and dryer — on purpose — and still he wore it for years. Sometimes I would threaten to wear my gardening shoes to dinner unless he changed his jacket.

I had bought him an expensive Italian suit in Houston. It was very conservative, navy blue — and he did love it. I just laughed. "I'm burying him in that navy blue suit." That should have been an easy decision, but I knew that he would probably want me to bury him in something old and take that wonderful suit and let somebody get some good out of it.

If you have never done it, it may be hard to imagine what it's like to walk into a roomful of caskets. They had several nice choices — bronze caskets, wood caskets — but one caught my eye immediately, because it was handsome, elegant, and so different. The funeral director said, "Now this one is really nice: It's steel." The girls and I looked at each other and laughed. I said, "That's it." John was in the steel business.

I didn't ask prices. After all, I had savings, and somehow it seemed disrespectful to John to think about costs, as if I were unwilling to pay for a nice funeral. His funeral cost just over $6,000. I was not shocked by this, because I had made arrangements when my mother died, and I had helped with arrangements for both my in-laws and my sister-in-law. So I was somewhat prepared for the costs.

I was surprised by the state paper's obituary policy of charging by the word. It was hard to decide what to include, because I couldn't remember many of his business and civic involvements. I couldn't remember some of his next of kin! We needed to include the names of the pallbearers, which we had not confirmed.

On and on. How many copies of the death certificate did we need? *Well, why do we need any?* I thought. *I know he's dead.* But you need them for social security, for the insurance companies, for probating the estate, and other reasons. I believe we settled on ten copies.

We worked on a memorial folder. What should it say? I chose my very favorite passage in the Bible, Psalm 121.

I will lift up mine eyes unto the hills,
from whence cometh my help.

My help cometh from the Lord,
which made heaven and earth.

He will not suffer thy foot to be moved:
he that keepeth thee will not slumber.

Behold, he that keepeth Israel
shall neither slumber nor sleep.

The Lord is thy keeper:
the Lord is thy shade upon thy right hand.

The sun shall not smite thee by day,
nor the moon by night.

The Lord shall preserve thee from all evil:
he shall preserve thy soul.

The Lord shall preserve thy going out and thy coming in
from this time forth, and even for evermore.

—Psalm 121

I knew where we would bury him—in a cemetery out in the country, about a mile from his home farm—but I didn't have a plot yet. When we got into this part of the planning, I was asked, "Who will call the grave diggers?" I didn't know you had to contact the cemetery. *Of course* somebody has to call them. Somebody has to pick the spot because they have to dig the hole. My brother-in-law Charles called for me.

We decided that the earliest we could have the funeral would be Tuesday because we were still notifying people. I wanted to get it behind me; I wanted to have the funeral as quickly as possible, early in the day. But there was already a service scheduled for Tuesday morning.

I remember very little about the rest of that day. I don't remember who was there, where we slept, what we ate. I remember I never got to be alone. I remember the phone was constantly ringing. The only thing I remember about Monday is that the construction crew showed up. Then I remembered we were adding on to the house.

I can't start dealing
with this yet;
I have to bury him first

Monday morning I heard some noises out back and realized the construction crew was back. I thought, *Somebody should have called them and told them not to come.* Then I realized there wasn't anybody else to call them; John would have been the one to do that. I sat in the house for a long time and watched them work, trying to decide how to tell them my husband was dead.

I went out in the back in my robe with my hair wet from the shower — it was early, about 6:45 — and I said, "Didn't somebody call you?"

I didn't know who to address. John had been the one to deal with them.

One of the workers said, "No."

"Well, my husband died," I said to no one in particular. It was the first time I had said those words.

He asked me to repeat it several times. "You mean Mr. Trusty, the one who owns this house?"

"Yes, my husband died. He had a heart attack Saturday."

I could see shock and disbelief on their faces. They were sub-contractors and John had been the one who dealt with them. I said, "I'll contact you later, but I'll need a few weeks." Lots of thoughts were racing through my mind.

I was sorry to send them away; they had driven from Conway, about an hour's drive from Russellville. I even considered allowing them to work that day, but I was already wondering: *Do I really want to finish this? Do I want to tear these beams down and fix the house back like it was?* I would no longer need the additional space, and now there was the financial consideration. I didn't even know if the beams had been paid for. I stood in my den and watched the foreman tell each of the workers. Each one fell silent as he heard the news. They gathered up their tools quietly, respectfully.

I knew how much we had borrowed for the project, but I didn't know how much we had spent. Then I began wondering what else I would have to pay for if I tore the building down. We had signed a contract for cabinetry Thursday or Friday. I went back in the house and called the cabinetmakers and asked them if they would cancel my contract because my husband had died. They were understanding and agreed to do so.

I began trying to determine what other things I would have to pay for — things that needed my immediate attention. If they had already started building the cabinets, I would have had to pay for them.

I called my general contractor and told him I wouldn't do anything until after the funeral. I told myself, *I can't start dealing with this yet; I have to bury him first.* Then I went on with preparations for the funeral.

At the funeral home, they asked me when we wanted to have the visitation. The visitation was one of the most confusing periods during those weeks. Although I had helped with the arrangements for my mother and my in-laws, I hadn't dealt with this. After all, there was a time when people didn't have visitation.

Later, people would say to me, "I'm so sorry I was unable to come to John's funeral." And I would think, *But you were there.* Or they would say, "I'm so sorry that I didn't make it to the wedding." Again, I thought, *I remember seeing you.* Even today, I get the visitation at the funeral home and the receiving line at the wedding mixed up.

At the visitation, we went into a small room with two doors, and they brought the people through. Jim Bob Humphrey, the funeral director, told me that between six hundred and eight hundred people came to that visitation. He came in several times and asked that we try and move a little faster because people were lined up outside and all down the block. Some were driving away.

It's hard to hurry some things. One of John's employees came up to me and said, "I was afraid to come in, so I drove around a

long time." He handed me a sympathy card—he was crying—
and he said, "I can't do anything for you. I would if I could. But I
wanted you to know that if it hadn't been for John Trusty, me and
my wife and my kids would have starved to death." I don't know
what John had done for him, other than give him a job. But I
guess by the look on my face, he thought he had upset me. He
started apologizing and I told him, "You'll never know what
you've given me." I thanked him. That was exactly what I wanted and needed to hear: that someone else cared for him, too.

I was overwhelmed by the number of people who came, and
how far some had driven. It was apparent our little church wasn't
going to be large enough to handle the crowd at his funeral. The
choice to have the service at some place other than our home
church was a difficult one, but I was beginning to realize I had
made the right decision.

The service was set for Tuesday afternoon at the First Baptist
Church in Russellville. (John and I had many close friends in that
church and a lot of respect for the pastor, Dr. Stephen Davis.)
John's favorite hymn was "Sweet Hour of Prayer." I asked that the
congregation sing that song, and our minister of music, Shawn
Crane, sang, "His Eye is on the Sparrow." I talked with our minister, Chuck Roach, about the kind of service I wanted. I wanted
everyone to leave his funeral with a sense of peace and comfort.

One of the more difficult moments was when they took us out
into the auditorium for the service. I wasn't familiar with the
church. When they ushered us out, I saw that we were at the front
of the church, and as we walked out, we were facing the crowd.
I was both touched and surprised to see so many people, but I
couldn't face them. I couldn't look at them.

John would not have wanted an open casket service. The casket was closed. Beside it we placed a family portrait we had had
made about a year before. For years, John had refused to have a
picture made. I had bargained with him: I would agree for him to
wear that old favorite jacket if he would agree to sit for the portrait.

After the service, as they ushered the people around, again I
was overwhelmed. I wanted so badly for John to know how much
people cared because it touched me to the depths of my being.

I have a recording of the service, and I have listened to it. It is very uplifting. Many people have told me, "You know, I dreaded his funeral; I didn't want to go, but when I left there, I just felt comforted." John would have wanted it that way.

John was buried in Ellsworth, a small, beautiful cemetery not far from his birthplace. Several people remarked, "This is absolutely beautiful; this is John." Since it's about forty-five miles from Russellville, I didn't expect many people to attend the graveside service. Driving down in the family car, Jonna was seated facing the back; I was facing forward. She said, "Mom, I want you to turn around and look." We were on a straight stretch of highway. For miles, as far as you could see, there were cars. You could not see the end of the procession.

I had given some very specific instructions for the burial. I didn't want us to be there when they lowered the casket. I didn't want to be there when they put the dirt back over the hole. I told them to wait until they took us away.

My daughters, their husbands, Jim Bob, and I got in the family car. We took a different route back to Russellville. We cut across the Scranton bridge. None of us had seen a restroom since the service had started hours ago. We stopped at a little roadside store. As we pulled into the parking lot, we were amused at the stares we were getting. It was obvious that limousines full of people were not an everyday occurrence around there, and they were all trying to see who we were. I remember thinking, *If they only knew*.

Our church family was incredible. Members prepared a huge dinner the night of the funeral for our family and friends. Several of the deacons went to the city council and requested, successfully, that the name of the street on which our church is located be changed to John Trusty Lane.

Two of the men in the church who were good friends of John's, Bill James and Gary Couch, mowed my lawn and cleaned my pool the rest of that summer. Their wives, Vicky and Kerri, good friends of mine, did everything right. One day, I asked them how they always knew just what to do and say. They confessed they had bought a book called *When Your Friend is Grieving* and had read it together. I was deeply touched.

The community response was also overwhelming. I knew that the next thing on the agenda should be thank-you notes. There were close to four hundred floral arrangements, page after page in the visitation registry, people who came to my home with food, books, or other expressions of sympathy. At the same time, wedding gifts were arriving. And I was numb.

My dear friend Linda Bewley came through again. I don't know what I would have done without her. She took charge of this major project. She set up card tables and organized crews to work on the thank-you notes. I wanted so badly to write each one personally. With over five hundred, I couldn't. But I didn't let any go out without my knowledge. I went through every one, organized them into stacks. I wrote different model letters for those who brought food, sent flowers, businesses, etc. They may not have had my handwriting, but they had my message.

Vicky and Kerri were still taking turns coming by. It was nearly three months before I had any private time, because when I told people I needed to be alone, they misunderstood and thought I wasn't doing well. I needed to cry, and I couldn't in front of anyone. They all meant so well. But finally, one day I said, "Don't come by today. I need to be alone."

John Trusty

John was born in an old farmhouse in Subiaco. He was the seventh son of the seventh son of the seventh son. His dad was a dairy farmer who reared him in a manner in which you can't rear children today. He would tell him, "Now, son, I don't care what time you come in, but at four o'clock in the morning your feet are going to hit the floor and we are going to the milk barn." He would get up at four o'clock and help his dad milk.

John was different. John was the baby of the family; he had six brothers and one sister. In our generation, about the worst thing you could get into was alcohol, but even about that, John was always the level-headed one: he was the driver.

John was a very complex and compartmentalized person. He had these little blocks and you got everything in your domain, but you didn't get anything in anybody else's. Including his: he had his own space. Every marriage has troubles, but the biggest problem we had was my trying to get to know him. For the first twenty years of our marriage I took it personally, but I finally decided, "This is John, this is his personality, this is not a fault. He gives me more than he gives anybody else. As much as he can give."

I knew him, and yet I never knew him. After he died, when people shared things with me they knew about him, I realized they knew a lot of things about him I didn't know, and that angered me at times. But sometimes it made me love him more.

One of my daughter's friends told me this story. We always took our kids and their friends on trips. This little girl spent a lot of time at our house and once we flew to Dallas to shop at the Galleria. John had given all the kids a fifty-dollar bill, and this little girl was so excited about it. She put her money in her shoe and, somehow, going through the mall, she lost it. She came back to the hotel crying. John came up to her and said, "Stacey, what's the matter?" She said, "I lost that money." He reached in his pocket and pulled out another one and said, "Don't cry; it's just money."

He walked around the corner and put quarters in the Coke machine and it wouldn't give him a Coke. He stood there and beat on it for a while; then he went to the desk and made them give him his quarters back. He would give you the shirt off his back, but if he thought you were trying to take him for a nickel, he wouldn't stand for it. John was a very, very generous person. I've had two of the waitresses at the Holiday Inn tell me he put them through school with generous tips.

John was kind, compassionate, a very caring person, a good father, a good son, a good brother, a good Christian. He loved doing for everybody else—but would never buy anything for himself.

He was a wonderful husband. He was a workaholic though—something that was very difficult for me to live with. It's true what they say: When you own your own business, it owns you. In our early years of marriage, I didn't understand that because for the most part I was left to raise the kids. There were times I felt he was unfair. Now when I look back, I see it differently. There is no one—

absolutely no one—who loves his children more than John loved his. But there were times when I would call him at eight o'clock when he still hadn't gotten home, and he would tell me, "I forgot to come home."

He would come home some days and say, "I love what I do; I love my job." I was glad he could feel that way. But in the later years when the business became more competitive, he was really looking forward to getting out. He wanted out.

The night before he died, someone had invited us out to dinner, but he was so tired that we stayed home. He fell asleep. The phone rang, and the answering machine answered. It was someone from Searcy Steel saying, "John, all the wheels have fallen off again. I think you ought to call me." But John didn't take the call; that wasn't like him. I said, "Aren't you going to call back?" And he said, "No." That was the first time I ever saw him ignore business. Now I wonder whether he was not feeling well that night. He got a total of three calls that Friday night about problems—a truck driver and two others—but he didn't take the calls. He said, "I'm not going to deal with it tonight. I'll deal with it Monday."

John was very supportive of me. He pushed me into doing things that were good for me. Even things I didn't want to do. He wanted me to be involved in politics. He wanted me to run for office. Once I had a leadership role in a political campaign and one of the guys said, "John, she's not barefoot and pregnant." John said, "I'll tell you what, I've had it both ways, and I'll take it this way." He was my biggest fan. We sometimes got letters to Mr. and Mrs. Sharon Trusty. Where some men might have been insecure, he thought it was funny. He was very secure, very trusting, always supportive. He never held me back; he brought out the best in me. This was also true with his children.

People make me happy. When my daughter went through her divorce, someone told me, "You're only as happy as your least happy child." When the people I love are around me and they're happy, I'm happy. Things don't make me happy. I am grateful and appreciative for things, but John made me happy. He was my happiness.

"Daddy, they're playing our song"

John died on Saturday, July 23, exactly two weeks before Jessica was to be married.

Before the wedding, I cancelled our trip to Japan. We were to go with our friend Jim Burnett. A Japanese aviation safety group was dedicating a monument to him; we were going over with some government dignitaries to be a part of the ceremony. We had planned to leave on Monday, after the wedding on Saturday. A lot of special arrangements had been made, and they had to be unmade. Jim made some calls and took care of it. The next thing was to call my contractor and tell him I would wait until after the wedding to do anything else with the house.

So after the funeral, I focused on the wedding. One of the first things to do was decide whether to go ahead with it. I left that up to Jessica. I was happy she had Robert, that she had a new love in her life. I felt it would help her get through her grief.

I could tell she was concerned it might be disrespectful to go ahead with the wedding. I thought I sensed she wanted to go ahead with it, but I was afraid I might be reading her wrong. So I said, "If you want to go ahead with it, your father would want you to." She said, "I want to go ahead and get married, but what will all the people think?" I said, "That's not a consideration."

Almost everything was in place. We had the caterer, the flowers, and the band. Our friends Bill and Janet Mitchener were to have the reception at their house. That had been the plan all along because of the construction on our house.

The day before John died, I had a call from Tom Bagby, the photographer, that Jessica's bridal portrait was in. I couldn't wait for her father to see it because he hadn't seen her in her dress. So I ran down and picked it up, and I went back home and hung it on the wall where he would be sure and see it when he came in that night. He walked over to the wall and looked at the picture for a long time. He said, "She is so beautiful." I was glad for Jessica that her dad had seen her in her bridal gown.

Giving his daughters away had never come easily for John. He had never been a very good father-of-the-bride. When Katherine had married, he balked at everything from wearing a cummerbund with his tuxedo to attending the parties. He was very traditional, and the young men his daughters married had to ask his permission. When Bruce had asked for Katherine's hand, John said, "I would say no, but you'd probably just do it anyway." Four years later, when Scot asked for Jonna's hand, John said the same thing.

After that wedding, when everyone had gone, John came into the den where I sat reading. He stood looking at me and then said, "I am never going to give Jessica away. Don't even ask me." And without another word he left the room.

Five years later, when Jessica was to be married, I remembered that statement. John Trusty was a man of his word, and I did not want to put him in the position of having to honor what he had said, so I never brought it up. I just assumed he would give her away when the time came and decided to leave the rest to the wedding director. Sometimes John Trusty was a very stubborn man.

The things I remember about the wedding are painful. I had submitted the information to the local newspaper, the Russellville *Courier,* ahead of time. I had to tell them to change "the daughter of John and Sharon Trusty" to "the daughter of Sharon Trusty and the late John Trusty." I changed the program. John had started writing a poem for Jessica — about "a little girl with the yellow curl who thinks Daddy knows it all." He hadn't finished it; but I added a few lines to it, and we put it on the back of the program. Jessica wanted that done.

Jessica said all her life she had known what she was going to say to her father. She was going to look up when the bridal march started and say, "Daddy, they're playing our song." I said, "You can do that anyway."

She decided to have my dad, her only living grandparent, walk her down the aisle. Then she said, "I think when the minister says, 'Who gives this woman?' I think we'll say, 'Her father and mother.'" John had liked Robert, so we decided we'd do that.

Next we had to decide who was going to escort me. Jessica did not want me to walk down the aisle alone. She wanted someone special to escort me. So I walked down the aisle with our dear friends Congressman John Paul Hammerschmidt and his wife, Virginia. Jessica was happy with that.

I have a picture taken at the wedding that I have never shown to Jessica. After the photographer had taken pictures of the bridesmaids and the groomsmen, he said, "OK, now the bride's parents!" In the picture he took of Jessica and me, she has this beautiful smile and tears are just running down her cheeks.

(The next week Tom came to our home and apologized. He said, "I have to apologize; I'm so accustomed to saying, 'OK, now, groom's parents; OK, now, bride's parents.'" He felt really badly about it.)

We had to think about the receiving line. At some point, it dawned on me there were going to be people at the wedding that we hadn't seen since the funeral. I didn't want them to come through the receiving line and say to us—but especially to her— "I'm so sorry about your father." So I went to the minister and I said, "I don't know how you are going to handle this, but I want people to know when they come through the receiving line that this is Jessica's day. This is a happy event. I wish they wouldn't say, 'I'm sorry about your father.'"

Jessica and I had checked into the Holiday Inn two days before the wedding. I wanted and needed some private time with her. I had to tend to some details of the wedding, and I didn't have control over anything at my house. People were so concerned about us, and meant so well. They were still coming over, expressing their sorrow over John's death, bringing food and flowers—and we needed to plan a wedding.

After the wedding, everybody started leaving the church for the reception. Jessica had ridden to the church with me, but, of course, she left in the limousine with Robert. When I came out of the church, I guess I had in the back of my mind that someone would be riding with me. I started looking around for John.

I realized that I would be driving myself—to my daughter's wedding reception. Shock, cold and electrical, swept over me again. That was the worst moment of the wedding for me. That was the state I was in when Congressman Hammerschmidt walked over to me. I don't know whether he sensed it, but he asked, "Do you have someone to ride with?" I just stood there, and without waiting for an answer, he said, "Well, you're coming with me." He and Virginia took me to the reception, and they stayed by my side throughout the evening.

John had what he considered to be his "lucky coin." It was an old Spanish shipwreck "piece of eight" that he had carried for years. He never went anywhere without it. Jessica wanted to "borrow" it and wear it in her shoe. I could tell she felt it would be a connection to her father.

For some reason, I knew it would be hard for her to give it back to me, and I knew it would be hard for her to leave me—even to go on her honeymoon. I asked one of her bridesmaids to get it from her when they helped her dress to leave.

As Jessica and Robert were running to the car to leave, she came over to me with that same look on her face that I had seen earlier at the photo session—big smile, tears streaming. She held out her hand and stood there. I looked at her hand, and there was the coin. I took it from her, and she left crying.

I went back to the hotel that night because I had to cry.

I wanted everything in my life back just like it had been

The funeral was behind us, and now the wedding was over. After any major event, there are always loose ends to tie up, so I began trying to sort through those details. In trying to figure out what to do next, I moved into the pattern that was to become my way of life for the next two and a half years. I began confusing and fragmenting myself: because I was tackling everything at once...because I was never able to finish anything...because I was always tying up loose ends...because I was tackling everything at once. A mad, vicious cycle.

There was too much to do, and I was responsible for all of it. For one thing, I had to decide whether to go on with the construction on the house. I didn't want to; I knew I didn't need that much room. I wanted everything in my life, including my house, back just like it had been.

I called Bill Mitchener—John's business partner and dear friend—and asked him to come out with my contractor and see what it would cost to tear down the steel beams, dig up the concrete, rebuild my deck, and put my house back just like it had been.

I was feeling the burden of a new debt. We had made only one payment. After John's death, I received a notice in the mail asking me whether I wanted to take out credit life on the mortgage. I remember thinking how ironic that was.

I started to look for a way to eliminate that payment. I thought maybe I could build the house back like it was. I knew I would take a hit, but I was willing to do it if I could afford to make the payments on the note. But Bill told me it would cost almost as much to do that as it would to finish the project. And, of course,

I would have to pay off the loan, and I wouldn't have anything to show for it. So the decision was made for me: I had to finish the house.

I made a decision to do two things: to finish the house, and to grieve. I gave myself one year to grieve. I was going to do it as a job. Any time I needed to grieve, I was going to grieve; and I was going to do whatever it took to get through this. And in one year I would be finished. That's exactly what I told myself and everybody: "In one year I will be through with this job of grief." Jessica said, "Mom, I don't think that's something you can just make up your mind to do and do it." I said, "Yeah, I can." That's how naive I was.

About six weeks after John died, I called the steel truss people to come out. When they came back, it took about a month for them to finish. The steel was a major part of the budget. I wondered whether John had already paid for it or what arrangements he had made. Slowly I realized we didn't have a budget. We had a loan, but we didn't have a budget.

That was often the way my husband liked to do business because he was financially secure. I was, too, as long as his paycheck was coming in. He figured out how much he needed to do something and then if he needed more, he wouldn't hesitate to cash in a CD or sell a lot or whatever it took. I realized then that maybe the loan wouldn't cover the construction project. So I determined from that point on to look at every expenditure.

I sat down with pad and pencil and wrote: DEBT ANALYSIS COMMITTEE: ME, MYSELF, AND I. I wanted as little debt as possible. I first had to determine what materials had been ordered. Did I need them? Did I have to keep them? Were they already paid for? Then I drew up a budget for the construction project based on the loan amount. My budget was to use as little as possible and still have a well-built house.

Everything was subject to review. Things like the windows, which had been delivered and for which the holes had been cut, I was locked into. Several other things I was able to change. For example, we had planned to put cedar shakes on the new part of the house because we had cedar shakes on the existing portion. It was going to be very expensive to do that. But the whole house needed a new roof, and I was able to re-roof my entire house with architectural shingles for less money than it would have taken to put cedar shakes on just the new part.

We had intended to remodel the whole interior, but I found a stopping place that I would not go beyond. I used Berber carpet instead of tile; one area that called for a see-through fireplace I was able to simplify. I spent only twenty percent of what we had originally contracted for on cabinets. I reviewed every decision from that point on and kept a running tab against the budget.

When the steel truss people were finished, I was ready for the general contractor to come back and help me get the project going. My attempts to get him back were unsuccessful. I don't know why. He had several other jobs going, but he had had those going before. He had several crews, but my job just seemed not to be a priority. Looking back, I think it may have been that he didn't know how to work for a woman. Maybe because of John's death he found it difficult to know what to say to me.

But he just ignored me. I would call him, and he would tell me he was going to be there, and then he wouldn't show up. I would find him on a job, have a talk with him, and he would send people to the house; they would stay for just a couple of hours and leave. I knew that he was doing that to pacify me.

I would say to him, "You need to get the wood people in here."

He'd say, "Well, they can't come 'til the sheetrock people finish."

"Get the sheetrock people."

"Well, they can't come until the tile people finish."

"Get the tile people!"

Everybody wanted to be last. I said to him many, many times, "Somebody has to be first." I wanted it over with, and I couldn't even get it going.

They tore out the outside wall where the new part was to connect to the old—and didn't come back. I had a $1,000 electric bill one month because the soffits weren't up and I was heating all of Russellville. I found him on another job and asked him if he would send some people over, but they didn't show up. Finally I got some other people on my own to come and put boards up.

My friends were asking me, "How do you stand this?" My

whole house was gutted, except for three rooms in the back—my "cave"—where I had moved all my furniture. I had not had a kitchen stove for over four months. There were beams, concrete floors, and boxes. I was too confused to know what to do and too tired to do it.

My dad tells me he came over one morning and found me in one of the rooms, sitting on the floor behind some boxes, eating a bowl of cereal. He asked me what I was doing and I told him, "I'm trying to eat, and I just want it all to go away."

I look back now and realize that I needed to grieve and I couldn't. I thought, "If they would just finish and leave, I could get on with this grief thing and be finished with it." That was what I thought—that this feeling of sadness and loneliness and pain would just go away if I could just do whatever. I didn't know what I should be doing—I just knew I wasn't doing it.

I began to realize something then that I've been struck by many times since and will probably continue to be struck by for the rest of my life: that if *I* don't do something, it won't be done. I thought, *If I don't do something about this, the year 2000 will be here and I won't have a kitchen stove.*

I was confused and exhausted. I began to perceive every decision I had to make as a confrontation. It just seemed as though in addition to having to make the decisions, I was continually having to convince people: "Yes, this is what I want to do." Everyone seemed to second-guess me. I just wanted to scream, "Yes, I know what I'm doing! This is what I want! It's my money!" I didn't have time to explain. And I no longer had the energy to be nice.

I can't describe the exhaustion that comes with grief. It's unlike any other exhaustion. I was grateful for it. One of the things sympathetic people asked me often was, "Are you sleeping?" Oh, yes, I was sleeping. I would go back to my "cave" at seven in the evening and sleep until six or seven the next morning. I remember it as a black period. I didn't even dream. It was sheer fatigue. Maybe it was shock.

People say that once you lose your mate you are never the same person. I think that's true. I had a very hard time bringing myself to fire that contractor. I thought, *This is not the kind of person I used to be, but this is the kind of person I have to be now. And the kind of person I have to be now is not even the kind of person that I want to be.*

My *perception* that every encounter was a confrontation and there really being a confrontation were two different things. With the first contractor, I knew it was going to have to *become* a confrontation if I got anything done. I was going to have to become more assertive, and I didn't want to. For instance, I came home one day, and there was a saw sitting on my new wood floor, with nothing underneath. They were sawing boards without an attachment to catch the sawdust. Inside my house! The contractor wasn't there, as usual, so I took care of it. People emptied concrete trucks in my yard; new materials were left in the rain to ruin. But I couldn't always be there.

I couldn't stand it any longer! There were other things that needed my attention — things like filing forty-eight pages of documentation for estate taxes.

———◆———

And I said, Oh that I had wings like a dove!
For then would I fly away and be at rest.
Lo, then would I wander far off,
and remain in the wilderness:
I would hasten my escape from
the windy storm and tempest.
—Psalm 55:6-88

Sometimes you just
have to go ahead and do it

I have always operated under the premise that you don't get rid of something until you're sure you have something better with which to replace it. The first thing I did was call Kevin Smoke, the general contractor who came in to finish the job. He said he could start in about a week or so. Before I did this, I went to my first contractor three times, and I was very firm. I asked if he wanted me to get someone else. I told him I had to have someone to oversee the project and get it done. I did that three times and each time he said, "No, I'll do it."

After Kevin accepted the job, I called the first contractor one night and told him I had hired someone else and that he needed to come get his equipment. It was really hard to do it, but I just couldn't deal with him any longer.

Incredibly, he said, "No, I'm coming back Monday."

I said, "It's too late; you've been telling me that for too long." When he protested, I told him, "You don't understand; I have already hired someone to finish the job and I want you to come get your things."

The next morning, the first contractor went to the building suppliers around town and told them not to allow me to charge anything to his account. He was never the most cordial person to deal with anyway. I should have made the decision to fire him several months before I did, and it should never have been hard for me to do, but I was emotionally and physically exhausted.

The new contractor, Kevin Smoke, was a godsend. He had lost a younger brother about two weeks after John died. Kevin was intuitive and was able to tell when I was having a bad day. He would sometimes say, "Sharon, would you like me to take care of that for you?" It was that way from the day he got there in March. The first week he got a magnum-size dumpster. We hired a couple of guys from a temporary service, and we spent the first week cleaning up my yard. That's how bad it was. Then they started on the house.

Kevin was reliable; he came every time he said he would. He would do anything I asked him to do. If I wanted him to pick out the materials, he would; if I didn't, he let me. He was also very good at estimating and figuring out ways to save me money. He was exactly what I needed. It only took about sixty days to wrap it up. We finished in late May of 1995.

There was still a lot of work to be done—those famous loose ends. My furniture was stacked in the back of the house. Everything was covered in sheetrock dust and sawdust. I didn't know what I was going to do. I didn't know who I could get to help with the heavy lifting—moving the furniture—and those things I couldn't do alone. But Kevin took care of that also. He told me, "Sharon, when I leave your house, it will be exactly like it was before you started this project." And it was. Even though moving the furniture was not his responsibility, he did it to help me.

I started the cleaning process and unloading boxes in an attempt to get my house—and my life—back in order. I came home one day to find Kirt Mosley from Home Furniture in Russellville up on a ladder, decorating my bookshelves, placing books, lamps, hanging pictures! He worked so hard. My old accessories looked wonderful. He got several people from Home Furniture to help move my piano, and he was there for all the heavy work. I was beginning to feel at home again. How could I not feel better with friends like these?

I continued to sleep in the old part of the house for over a month. I just couldn't move to my new bedroom. I wasn't ready. Then one Sunday at church my friends Bill and Vicki and Kerri and Gary said, "We're coming over and we're moving you." I said to myself, *Well, let them try.*

They carried all my clothes down to the new bedroom and moved me into it. That was the best night I'd had since John died.

One thing I've realized is that if you wait for it to be "time" to do something, it may never be time. You just have to go ahead and do it, and then after it's done, you realize that it *was* time. I probably never would have felt it was time to move to the new part of the house, but once I did it I realized I should have done it sooner.

I never felt like it was time to get rid of John's clothes. Jonna came and did that, and after it was done it was good. So now when I find myself waiting to be ready to do something, I consider these things, and sometimes I just go ahead.

I didn't feel angry with John for leaving me with the situation, but I was angry with the situation. What kept me from getting angry with John was that I knew he would never have left me with a mess. When he was dying, he had tried to say something to me. I believe he may have been trying to say something like, "Oh, I am so sorry that you have the wedding and that house mess."

Loneliness is no longer being the most important person in the world to someone

While the house was being completed, I desperately needed for it to be finished. I frequently complained that I needed privacy. After all, the year I had given myself to grieve would soon be up and I wasn't finished.

But as the house neared completion, I realized I wouldn't have workers there at seven o'clock every morning. They had been my reason for getting up. They had provided the structure for my life.

Structure is important for anyone, and I had always had it — in the form of working, or getting John off to work, or my children off to school. And I realized that for the first time in almost thirty-two years I would be by myself. That scared me to death. It brought feelings of both loneliness and of being alone. There is a difference.

Being alone is when the particular type of support you need is not there, or when you perceive it's not there. For example, in business I was alone because no one had the kind of investment in my life that John and I had. I asked myself how I could rely on anyone to give me advice when those decisions are a lot less important to them than they are to me. With John, things like that had been equally important to both of us.

Loneliness is no longer being the most important person in the world to someone. Not ever hearing your name called in the house. One night, a few months after John died, I realized I hadn't heard anyone say "Sharon, I'm home." I just called his name: "John!" Then I called my name. I realized I hadn't heard anyone calling my name like that in months.

I'm basically a creature of habit, but for the first year or so, I slept on John's side of the bed. I remember right after he died I had a back problem, and one night I slept with a heating pad. I cannot tell you the feeling I had when I rolled over in the night and there was a warm spot in the bed. I slept with that heating pad for a month. That's loneliness. The fact that nobody was going to be there made me feel both — alone and lonely.

At this point I started looking at my life to determine what I needed to do next, what I had put on the back burner. What would I do for structure? I had millions of things to do. I just didn't want to do them.

For one thing, there were financial matters. I had a capable business partner who was taking care of what was still to me my husband's business. But I hadn't begun to wrestle with the reality of my finances. Maybe if I had been able to grasp what my future responsibilities were going to be, I would have gone in a different direction. But I have this great need to nurture. People have always said that I am a "fix-it" person. Which, I think, is why I did the next thing that I did.

Our local state senator, Lu Hardin, had announced that he was not going to run for re-election; instead he planned to run for the U.S. Senate. That left an open seat. John and I had always been involved in politics, and he had always wanted me to run for office. It had never appealed to me. But for some reason — maybe because I'd been involved as a volunteer — people thought I entertained this notion. I started getting calls encouraging me to run for the state senate seat, and I just said, "No, thank you." This was about a year and a half after John died — about the time the house project was nearing completion. I didn't even flatter myself enough to think they were serious.

The person who changed my point of view was my dear friend Jim Burnett. He said, "Sharon, you don't even have to make up your mind for a year." He continued, "Just don't burn any bridges or close any doors." As a Christian, over the years I've attempted to allow God to direct my life and take me where he wants me to go. Especially since John's death, I have called on him to guide me. I had been praying about open doors. I said to God, "If this is a door you have opened, you are going to have to make me want to do it — because I don't want to."

Then one day I woke up with a feeling of anticipation, and I realized it was that race. No one was more shocked than I was. I couldn't believe I was excited over running for political office. I didn't tell anyone for a while because I wanted to be able to back out if the feeling passed, which I was sure it would. But it didn't; it just grew more intense. I didn't really feel that I wanted to run for office, but I wanted to serve. I made the decision to do it.

I ran as a Republican. This race proved to be one of the best experiences of my life. I realized going in that I might not win. I thought I would; I knew I could. I entered the race accepting that whatever happened was what was meant to be. That didn't mean I worked less or didn't put my whole self into it. But, in fact, with my need to nurture and my fix-it nature, the district would have been well served had I won.

I became very possessive about the district as I traveled around. And I loved the people. In Paris, Arkansas, I met an elderly gentleman named Mr. Nixon who said, "Lady, I'm the biggest Democrat in Logan County." I said, "Well then, Mr. Nixon, you are just the person I want to talk to. I need new votes." We talked for a while, and he gave me a dollar. (I still have it.) He said he would vote for me.

Then there was a little lady in her seventies who had opened a Christian bookstore. She was so successful she was moving to a new location. But I met other senior citizens who were working two jobs because social security wasn't enough, and that broke my heart. By the time the campaign was over, I wanted to help everybody. If I had time today, I would drive over the district, to the little stores and gas stations, just to visit with the people because I really learned from all of them. I've always had a great faith in people, but this reinforced my feeling. I lost the race 48 percent to 52 percent. That loss paled in comparison to what came next.

Our family was just beginning to function as a unit again when Jessica and Robert separated. We all loved Robert. I was very concerned for both of them. My complete helplessness to fix their marriage was the most difficult thing I had faced since John's death. When the crisis is me, my children are there for me; but when the crisis is my children, then I feel alone.

Jessica and Robert have divorced; they have an amicable relationship, and they've both started rebuilding their lives. But losing Robert was devastating for my family.

Again I postponed dealing with my business and financial matters. I was on a downward spiral that would finally lead me to action.

A widow has twice the work with half the staff

There's a major learning curve to being a widow. It takes a lot of time and effort. You have to learn how to start a lawn mower, thread a weedeater, replace vacuum cleaner belts, take down light fixtures to change the bulbs. You have to remember to change the oil every three thousand miles and rotate the tires every other oil change. Little things that take a lot of time.

My time during this period was consumed with learning. It was also during this time that my patience began to wear thin with my friends whose patience with *me* was wearing thin. There were people who said to me, "You know other people have been through this, and they are over it by now. Get on with the program."

Almost everybody seemed to think I needed more to do. Everybody had a solution: "Keep busy." "Do volunteer work." "Go to movies." "Have lunch." "You've got to get out more."

I didn't need more to do! I needed a friend who realized I didn't need more to do. Someone who would come over and say, "Let me help you do this or that." I lost some friends because I didn't have time to do what they thought I should be able to do.

Sometimes well-meaning friends would say, "Take time for yourself, Sharon." It was true that I was burning the candle at both ends. Keeping busy does help, but it doesn't matter if you keep busy until three in the morning: you are still alone. If you quit at three in the morning and you are alone, why not quit at ten at night?

My perception of my life at this time was that the kitchen sink would be stopped up, the car would be out of gas. These are things that you don't have anybody to take care of and they don't wait.

You haven't had time to go the bank,
you have no cash,
you're getting close to being overdrawn,
your CD matured last week,
and it's going to automatically renew at four percent.
Your eighty-three-year-old father has the flu,
you have disconnect notices from the electric company
because you haven't had time to pay the bills.

OK, what are you going to do? Go to a movie?

Honestly at this point in my life, every day was like that. A widow has twice the work with half the staff. In earlier years, I had been guilty of being one of the people at church who would say, "Let that little widow lady do it; she needs to keep busy." But I don't think that way any longer. In fact I try to help them.

Through the children's divorce, my dearest friend in the world was Bob Taylor, Robert's dad. He wanted what was best for Jessica and for Robert, just as I did. Bob would call me and in thirty seconds be able to tell what frame of mind I was in. Sometimes he would say, "Is Patty Pity at your house again?" It would sometimes make me think about what I was doing, but sometimes I would say, "Yeah, she's here, and she's going to spend the night, and we are going to have the biggest pity party you've ever seen. And we're going to enjoy every minute of it!"

After two and a half years, I was beginning to have great big pity parties — often. And I had this anxiety and this sense of urgency and all these emotions I couldn't quite put my finger on — it took a lot of sorting for me to identify — and it all related to my business matters.

I realized my unrest stemmed from not knowing the financial impact John's death would have on my long range future. I had already discovered that the plans we had made would not work any longer because they were based on the assumption we were both going to be alive. For example, retirement: I had married my social security only to learn that a widow can't draw her husband's social security until she is sixty. At forty-eight, I was too *young* for something!

I needed to make some decisions that weren't based on what

John and I had planned, and I had postponed making those decisions because I had some resources other than social security. But I realized that thus far, I had exercised no stewardship of those resources.

I realized everything
seemed unfamiliar

Friends had been telling me for a long time that they were worried about me, but I didn't pay any attention. They told me I was being alone too much, and I would reply that I was dealing with it my own way, that we all deal with grief differently. But I heard that comment so often that I finally asked one friend exactly what she meant. She had the courage to tell me, "You're not acting right."

I began to understand what they meant when it occurred to me I didn't want to be around my children and they didn't want to be around me. When you don't want to be around your friends for a while, that's one thing. But I was avoiding my kids, and when I tried to talk myself out of it, I wasn't able to. I never told them I felt that way, but it must have been obvious: they would come over and I wouldn't answer the door. They would invite me to come to their homes or out to eat, and I would make excuses.

Soon I began to notice physical symptoms—dizzy spells, double vision, blurred vision. Then I couldn't remember things. For instance, I went to see my granddaughter Rebecca and I had forgotten she had started kindergarten. One day I was in the Copper Pig in the shopping mall in Russellville, and I realized I couldn't remember where the door was! The salesclerk asked, "Mrs. Trusty, can I help you with something else?" I was too embarrassed to say, "Where's the door?" So I just walked around the edges until I found it, and I went out into the mall.

When I got to the car, I realized that *everything* seemed unfamiliar, and that was what was wrong.

I began to realize that the reason I didn't want my kids around was because I thought I had to be strong around them—and it was just too hard to be strong. People told me it would be OK to cry in front of the girls, but I couldn't do it — and I still can't. The few times I have, it seemed to upset them, and that made me feel even worse. It was easier for me to just stay home and not try to be strong. So that's what I did.

I went to see my physician, Dr. Teeter, and he gave me a clean bill of health. When I told him about my surrealistic episodes, he said, "I think you are just stressed, Sharon. I think it is grief and stress." He said he thought I might benefit from some counseling.

I was having what I later learned are "counterfeit feelings" — one feeling built on another, built on another, built on another. I began to feel guilty because I was afraid I was making my children feel they had lost both their mother and their father. And I became afraid something would happen to one of them — that one of them would need me — and I wouldn't know it. If I had to run to town to do an errand, I would run back home and check the answering machine. Then I would run back to town and do another errand and run back home and check the answering machine again — in case one of them needed me.

I wasn't sleeping well. I would dream I was searching for John. I would be in the kitchen and someone would say, "John just went into the bedroom" and I would run in there and someone would say, "Oh John just left," and I would get in the car and go searching for him.

I also dreamt I was falling, and just before I hit bottom I would wake up, startled, and then, like ice cold water, remember he was dead. I would wake up several times a night like that.

So I quit going to bed. I would just stay up all night and work. It didn't bother me; I wouldn't even be sleepy the next day. I would tell myself, "If I can't control my emotions, at least I can control my body." I would sometimes go two days and two nights without sleep and just work. Then I would crash.

I was too involved in what I thought of as "taking care of business" to focus on those things that could heal. I did what everyone told me to do: I stayed busy. I always had a list of things I needed to get done; I never got them finished. I was operating in an overload mode. I knew I couldn't do that forever, but

I told myself I could until I got through it.

But it was becoming obvious to me: I wasn't going to get through it. When I discussed this with some close friends, they told me I needed to go talk to someone. So after reading every book I could find — and talking with my doctor and with friends — I thought, "If I had a toothache, I would hire someone to fix it; if I had a flat tire, I would hire someone to fix it." I decided then and there I was going to have to hire someone to fix my emotions.

"Sharon, honey, I don't think you are where you think you are"

When John died, Jim Bob Humphrey, the funeral director, gave me a little book about losing someone you loved. Several months later, the funeral home offered a grief therapy class. I didn't know how group therapy worked. I knew I didn't want to share my pain with strangers. But the book had helped me so much that I thought maybe I could just listen, and maybe I could also find out what books other people were reading that had helped them.

The first session was held in a local church. I was very nervous, and when I drove by and saw that the parking lot was full of cars, I considered going back home. Then I spotted a friend, Una Hankins, and thought, *Oh, good.* I parked the car, and when I got out I noticed she was carrying a covered dish for potluck. She said, "I'm so glad you came."

Inside there were about eighty people who seemed to be having the best time, and there was all this food. *Hmmm, they sure are happy*, I thought. As I signed in, I asked a woman, "Is this the grief therapy class?" She assured me it was. So I sat down. I began to see other people I knew. A woman sat down next to me, and I asked her whether she had ever been to one of these meetings before. She said, "Oh yes, honey; I've been coming for a year." I thought, *Well, that's why she's happy*.

Una was sitting behind me and she said, "Sharon, honey, I don't think you are where you think you are."

I turned around and said, "But they say that's normal."

"No, I mean aren't you wanting that six-week course in grief management?"

"Yes."

And she said, "Honey, this is the singles group."

I nearly started to cry. The program had begun. When I started climbing out over all these people, they said, "Aw c'mon stay, Sharon. It'll be OK." But I went on out, and I cut across the parking lot to where the grief therapy class was supposed to be. I opened this door, and there were about eight or ten elderly people there.

The next day I called my girls and said, "You'll be proud of me; I went to a singles group last night." They said, "Good for you, Mom!"

But I didn't go back to the singles group. I did go about six times to the grief therapy group. I just listened, and it was helpful. At first, I was the youngest one there. Later, a younger woman joined whose husband had died of cancer. Then there were two more ladies, and the group grew to about twenty. I was the only one in that group who had lost a spouse to sudden death. The others had all lost loved ones after long illnesses.

Linda Polk, Emmelene Kerr, Brenda Weaver, and I started meeting for dinner before the group meetings. Emmelene had lost her husband about a year before the rest of us, and she had become active in the Widowed Persons' Services. She was a good resource for all of us, and we quickly bonded. As we became closer, we began to share more of our personal circumstances. Each of us, we discovered, had questions about financial issues. Our situations were vastly different, but we had something important in common. None of us knew exactly what to do about our future.

I had seen the Beardstown Ladies' Investment Club on the *Today* show. I suggested to the others that we start an investment club so we could learn together. We began looking for other interested people and eventually started the Arkansas Valley Investment Club with eighteen members.

The club helped me learn about money matters, but at the same time I began to realize just how much I didn't know. For example, one of the members shared her story with us. She was entitled to her husband's retirement account. She had two options: one, take the money in a lump sum, invest it, and live off the interest; or two, receive a fixed monthly income check from the retirement account. She hadn't known how to make that decision and had gone to a financial consultant who advised her to take the money in one lump sum and invest it. She confided to us she had done what he suggested and was now receiving more monthly income from interest on investments than her monthly check would have amounted to — and her portfolio had increased $80,000 in one year! She had more monthly income and still had all of her principal.

I began to realize the magnitude of some of the decisions I was going to have to make. I was becoming even more anxious now, feeling there wasn't enough time to learn everything I needed to know before I would have to make those decisions. I had been trying to hurry up and grieve, and now I needed to hurry up and learn.

You can't buy bread
with a piece of steel

When John died, Bill not only lost a partner, he also lost a friend. Many people have commented over the years that their partnership was unique. They complemented each other in their abilities to run a business. They were a great team. And they were the best of friends.

At the time of John's death, each had more to do than he could get done. Bill had undergone open-heart surgery not long before John died. When John died, he suddenly found himself having to run Searcy Steel, about 100 miles away, while he was also running the business in Russellville. I knew he was stressed, and I didn't want to add to his stress. I didn't want him to think, *Here's John's wife—again.*

I was pretty sure Bill hadn't planned to be in business with his partner's wife. But we met often and discussed business. My goal at the time may have been misguided: I was simply trying to *not* cause problems for Bill. He was running the company, and I didn't know whether he knew me well enough to know that I didn't intend to tell him how to do it. It was obvious to me he was trying hard to see I was taken care of. But with all his other responsibilities, I was beginning to understand that this arrangement needed reassessment. It wasn't supposed to be Bill's responsibility to take care of me for the rest of my life.

My perception had been that I was taking care of my personal business, getting my life under control. But I began to realize what was keeping me so busy was "make-work." It wasn't that I didn't have enough to do; I just didn't want to do what really needed to be done. I was taking care of things I was familiar with, things I knew how to do. But the time had come for me to make some major decisions about my future. What I would need was information — a lot of it.

I had so much to learn before I could make the decisions I needed to make. It was going to take a lot of my time to learn it, and a lot of someone's time to teach me. I knew Bill didn't have that kind of time. Besides, my goal was to begin accepting responsibility for myself. I began to ponder who would be willing to help me learn. I needed someone to bring wisdom and insight to the situation.

Decisions. Information. Lack of information. John had life insurance policies through the business. I didn't have those proceeds yet; I had been living out of savings. I began to worry about "eating too much of my seed corn." After all, my husband had left me assets. I held interests in several companies, several pieces of commercial real estate, and other things of value. John and I had made provisions for ourselves. We had drawn up wills so that when one of us died, our assets transferred to the survivor.

But you can't buy bread with a piece of steel, and you can't make the house payment with a lakefront lot. I needed cash.

I negotiated some arrangements with Bill on mutually owned properties that yielded some cash with which to pay some debts, and this helped decrease my monthly budget needs. I really didn't know what I was doing, and I was fortunate that Bill is an honest person.

But there was still the issue of a paycheck. By this time, I was beginning to feel like a charity case. I've always had confidence in my ability to manage money, and I've always been good at budgeting. But without information, I couldn't determine what the budget would be — or how much there would be to budget with.

John and Bill had started working on an ESOP — an Employee Stock Option Plan — before John died. An ESOP is a process whereby the employees of a company acquire from the owners stock in the company, and at that time I didn't know how his death would affect the outworking of the ESOP. John and Bill had planned to sell the company through ESOP and retire. I wasn't even sure we could proceed with it.

John had two life insurance policies through the business. The first policy had been set up between a trust and our company. The death benefit was to be paid when the second of us died in order to pay estate taxes. There was no death benefit that I could use for my income. John and I had discussed who would pay the premium, which was several thousand dollars each year. It was our understanding that Russellville Steel Company would pay them. The decision by the company to stop paying the premiums after John's death was disappointing. That decision was beyond my control. The second policy was to be paid directly to me at John's death. We had planned on it as the major source of funds for my needs. But the proceeds from the second policy were paid to the company. Then the company paid me a monthly check as taxable salary until the proceeds of the policy were gone. This resulted in my having to pay income tax on the proceeds of John's life insurance! I didn't get what John and I had counted on.

I didn't know what properties to sell, what to keep. I didn't want to make these decisions without understanding the consequences. I couldn't plan my future and I didn't know where I was going from there. The ESOP plan was on hold. Ideally, it would have been completed by the time the insurance proceeds ran out, but as time went on, it became obvious it wasn't going to happen. I knew the monthly check from Russellville Steel for the insurance proceeds would be coming to an end, but I couldn't really focus on what to do about it. I was confused about what had happened and what was going to happen within the planned time frame. When I sought information, I was met with resistance.

I didn't want people making the decisions they were making for me. When someone makes a decision *for* you, they take away all of your options. After all, my future couldn't be as important to them as it was to me. But I didn't have the time, energy, or emotional resources to take charge. Yet. When I did, I was surprised at what I discovered.

I had to find someone who didn't see me as just "John Trusty's widow"

It had taken nearly three years, but I was beginning to realize that John's assets were now my assets, that his business was my business. Everything that had belonged to John had become mine when he died. He wanted it that way. It was his last will and testament.

It took me a while to figure out what was happening. For the most part, people who were advising me during this time were people who knew us as a couple. And while my circumstances were now completely different, they were advising me based on what my circumstances once were. I had to get out of that mode of making decisions based on "John and Sharon Trusty." In order to do that I had to find someone who didn't know John Trusty or see me as just "John Trusty's widow."

I was distraught at not having a better understanding of business matters. I started with the ESOP plan. I pored over documents for months until I admitted to myself I didn't understand them. I moved on to the rental property, which was easier, but still, there were decisions that I didn't know how to make. The apartments needed repair work, which would eat up about six months' rental income. Should I make that investment, or should I sell? I couldn't decide, so I just went on to another piece of property with the same results. One of my tenants wanted me to remodel the piece of property he was renting so he could put in an automotive business. Then he decided he wanted to buy it. Then he wanted to know whether I would carry the note, whether he needed to go to the bank, whether we could do a long-term lease. I didn't know about that either, so I just went on to the next piece.

I had been unable to identify anyone who would sit down with me and explain all the considerations involved in making these decisions. But I realized something important: the more information I had, the better I understood. The better I understood, the clearer things were, the more confident I was, and the easier my life would be. I knew I had to get an understanding of it all.

One night I was having one of my very finest Patty Pity parties, and my friend Jim Burnett dropped by and caught me. I told him what was going on with me. He said, "Sharon, do you want me to give you the name of a person I have referred several people to?" And he referred me to a financial consultant.

I had been trying for a long time to do everything at once rather than focus on one manageable block of something. I was confused. I was coming unglued.

When Jim Burnett dropped by and found me in this state, I told him I didn't know what to do or where to turn: "Jim, I'm not expecting too much, am I? I *need* to understand my circumstances." I explained to him what I was seeking to accomplish. "It's been nearly three years since John died, and I am no further along in knowing about my future, or in getting prepared for retirement than I was the day he died!" Although well-meaning people were willing to accept responsibilities for me, I was too young to allow someone else to handle my financial matters for me. What they were saying to me was neither enlightening nor reassuring: "Let me take care of that." "Don't worry about that." "You don't have to know all that." I *wanted* to know.

When I asked questions—keep in mind I was dealing with friends—friends were offended. They didn't realize that I was now ready to assume responsibility for my life, that I *was* thinking clearly, that there was no lack of trust on my part. Some people still haven't understood why I sought outside help. I sought outside help not because I lacked confidence in the people I was working with, but because they lacked confidence in me.

You don't have to
have a lot of money
to learn or to plan

In truth, I didn't know what a financial consultant did. For that matter, I didn't know what roles a stockbroker, CPA, trust officer and others played. Had I known what services a financial consultant provided, I would have realized that this was the kind of advisor I needed. But I thought you had to have a lot of money before you needed a financial consultant. It's important to remember that a financial consultant helps you *learn* and *plan*. You don't have to have a lot of money to do that.

I had been using several different people for different areas of expertise, but none of it was meshing, partially due to the turf issues that surface when you deal with more than one person. When Jim said, "There is a financial consultant in Little Rock to whom I have referred several clients," he also gave me the name of a reference: "Do you remember Jeff Smith?" John and I had traveled to Washington in 1981 with a group that included Jeff and his wife, Lisa. Jim said, "I know Jeff wouldn't mind if you called him." So I wrote his number down.

I believe in Divine Providence. The next day I was in a shopping mall in Little Rock, and a man I didn't recognize came up to me and said, "Aren't you Sharon Trusty?"

"Yes, I am," I said.

"I know you don't remember me," he said, "but I'm Jeff Smith."

"I do remember you; we went to Washington together seventeen years ago," I replied. We talked and before he left, I said, "You know, it's really strange that we ran into one another because I was going to call you later in the week. Jim Burnett told me you have used a financial consultant named Barry Corkern, and that I might be able to talk with you about him."

Jeff said, "Oh, yes," and he was very complimentary of Barry.

That's how I found Barry. I went home, called his office, and made an appointment.

When I first met Barry, I was desperate for someone who could and would help me see the whole picture. I needed someone to explain my options and discuss the consequences of my decisions and choices. Until that time, when I had asked for advice, people had only said, "This is what you ought to do." No one talked about options or about *why* I should make the particular decision they were advising. I told Barry that I didn't want him to tell me what to do, that I didn't want anyone making decisions for me. You can find people who will make the decisions for you if that's what you want. That was not what I wanted.

When I went to see Barry the second time, I took some of my papers to him in a laundry basket—there were so many. As he picked up each document, he would explain it to me. The things that I had been looking at for weeks without being able to make sense of them, he was able to review and clarify for me. It didn't take me long to decide that I could work with him.

The first thing he advised me to do was so simple and so obvious, yet I had missed it. He told me to gather up the titles and deeds to everything that I owned. That one task simplified things and put my situation in perspective. I realized why I had been overwhelmed and confused: some of my papers were in my own safety deposit box, some with the accountant, some with my business partner, some in the corporate lock box, and some at the courthouse. Once I had all of them in my possession, what I was dealing with became tangible.

By this time, part of the ESOP sale of Russellville Steel had gone through. I had a certificate of deposit from the proceeds, but the bank was holding it as collateral, and I didn't have anything to show that the money would be mine someday. Barry told me to insist the bank give me a copy; I hadn't even realized I needed one. I had to ask the bank repeatedly. It took months to get it. I hadn't known what my rights were, but I was beginning to find out.

Writer Thomas Szasz once observed that you have to be humble to learn. I was going to have to be responsible for me for the rest of my life. There were a lot of things I needed to learn. I was beginning to be humble.

Coming out of Confusion

---◆---

Barry:
*A widow always needs
a good, objective advisor —
a decision partner.*

"What do I do now?"

It's not uncommon for my new clients to come to my office completely disorganized. But even so, there were significant questions that Sharon was unable to answer. As she told me about events that were taking place, decisions being made, actions being taken, I became alarmed. A widow, or any other survivor, can't assume that everything being done in her behalf is in her best interest.

I realized immediately there was a lot of work to be done. I knew I could be of help to Sharon, and she saw that I was not like the other people she had tried to work with before.

But I didn't know if she would return to my office. A client cannot engage me on the first visit. Regulations for investment advisors prevent a new client from entering into a formal arrangement any sooner than two days after the first meeting. This rule creates an environment that is conducive to getting to know a person before you work with them. Both the advisor and the client must be free and comfortable to discuss anything. I think that really comes through when the first meeting ends without a commitment, without signing any documents, without writing a check or taking any action. The first visit lets the client describe the situation and gives me a chance to determine if I can help in any way.

We are all a culmination of our life experiences. My past has molded me to be the consultant I am. My career began when I was twenty-three years old. I had been going to college at the University of Arkansas as a political science/pre-law major. I wanted to be an attorney, but in the '60s it wasn't cool to want to be a corporate attorney.

To tell the truth, I couldn't decide what I wanted to do. I was working part-time in a shoe store to supplement student loans. I quit going to school, and they gave me a full-time job. Eventually I managed two or three of their shoe stores. And a funny thing happened: business became interesting to me. I was frustrated: I hadn't finished college, but now I wanted a professional career. I responded to a classified ad for The Prudential Insurance Company, and I eventually went to work for them. The company would allow me to continue to take courses and get my education, and there was more opportunity for advancement.

As a new agent I was given a debit agency, which is like an established clientele. Decades ago, the agent would go by the policy owner's home or workplace each week and collect the premium. We collected premiums monthly; my debit was the southern part of Fayetteville and extended out into the countryside down to Greenland.

The other agents who worked for Prudential were great guys. I was moving out of an environment with no direction or future to one that had a structure and a purpose. I had drive. I had a tremendous thirst for knowledge, and I quickly developed the reputation for asking too many questions. While I was studying for the exams to get my license, I would ask, "What if this happens? What if that happens?" They would just tell me, "You're thinking too much."

During my first week my manager said, "We have to deliver this death benefit to someone on your debit." An astonishing number of policies never mature as a death benefit because people drop the insurance. Many insurance agents have gone through long careers and never delivered a death benefit check.

My manager was a guy named Ward Adams who had a fondness for smoking pipes and listening to bluegrass music. That day we loaded up in his car and drove to Greenland, continued south down U.S. Highway 71 until we came to a gravel road that turned off to the left. We continued until we came to a very modest country home — you know the kind of home, behind schedule for paint and repairs, one that over many years had held the laughter of children, grandchildren, and friends. Decades of Christmas and Thanksgiving dinners had been served there. It was the home of an aging couple who had just wanted to make ends meet until it was their time to go.

I was nervous. I was a brand-new agent and didn't know much about what we were doing. I was only twenty-three years old and had no experience with death, with grief. I didn't know what to expect. We had called for an appointment; the widow's daughter, who appeared to be in her mid-thirties, answered the door and invited us in.

I can't remember the widow's face, but she must have been in her sixties. She was devastated—lost and confused. Her future and finances were clearly in doubt. We needed to talk about something with which she was familiar. So I asked her to tell me about her husband.

Ward was a good-hearted guy, but he seemed awkward in this situation. He looked at me as if I had put my foot in my mouth. But it was quickly evident that she *wanted* to talk about her husband. She felt comfortable talking about her life's mate. Talking about him made me feel more comfortable too.

An important thing for me was that in the course of the conversation I learned that the insurance proceeds weren't going to be enough. I don't remember the exact amount of the check; I want to say that it was somewhere around five or six thousand dollars. Back in 1973 that was a pretty decent amount of money. But for somebody like her, it wasn't enough to live on for the rest of her life. So I left there knowing something about the person who had passed away, observing the widow's grief and confusion—and knowing she wasn't going to have enough to live on.

The insurance, although theoretically a good idea, had failed her. There wasn't enough money, and she was confused. I remember that first event more vividly than I remember the subsequent ones. I had two more occasions where I delivered checks—and I worked in that office only two years before I was promoted to sales manager and moved to Little Rock. But I still remember those guys commenting, "You have delivered more death benefit checks than I have, and I have worked for Prudential for years."

In each one of those cases I took the time to ask the widow: "Tell me about your husband." In each of those cases the widow was frustrated and confused, and in each of those cases there wasn't enough money. Seeing this in my twenties—observing the grief and confusion, and knowing in each case there wasn't enough money—had a profound impact on me. Ultimately, it drove me to leave the insurance business.

In overall financial planning, you analyze all your client's assets. Insurance is not the answer for everything. In the work I do now, insurance is sometimes a component, a part of the answer, but not all the answer. I found it frustrating knowing, as I gained education and experience, that the insurance I was selling was solving only part of the puzzle.

Almost all the nine guys I supervised as sales manager were old enough to be my father. This staff had not been doing very well. I trained them to do quality work so that when somebody bought an insurance policy, they didn't drop it. I taught my agents: "Here's the reason people buy insurance; here's the process we take them through so they can make informed decisions. We are not putting little wooden caskets on the table while we're making sales pitches. Our clients will feel they are making good decisions based on the good information we give them. Because we do want these people to have insurance when they die, especially young people who have children." So we had the confidence that when we sold insurance it would be kept by the client.

We had the lowest lapse rate in the region and ended up in the top fifteen percent of all of Prudential for two years. And that was important to me.

I managed the staff for five years. It was like having a twenty-year career crammed into five. I was increasingly frustrated with not being able to work in other financial areas. I would review a situation and analyze it, but I couldn't discuss tax or investment or capital structure of businesses or all the other financial areas that needed to be addressed. And I didn't see anybody out there pulling together the accountant, the attorney, the banker, the trust officer, the stockbroker, the insurance agent, the real estate agent—all these different experts—to help the clients make good financial decisions with long-term rather that short-term perspectives.

So I changed careers in 1980. Changing from insurance to financial planning was, I believe, as big a leap as if I had changed to driving a truck. Insurance and financial planning are completely different businesses.

I started my own practice in 1982. One of my first clients was a man named Carroll Plumlee. He and his partner had a trenching business; they buried cable for Southwestern Bell. It was a profitable business. His partner was older than he and planned to retire sooner. Carroll was saving some money; he and his partner had set up a little retirement plan, but they hadn't managed the investments very well. He had a son who didn't plan on taking over the business; his wife, Gloria, taught school.

Carroll had never met someone like me who could review every detail and then say, "OK, here are the strategies we should consider in your business and your personal financial life." He was the ideal client. I don't have the objective of going out and becoming a friend to my client, but it's impossible to work with somebody without caring for them. You discover problems; you help them solve problems; you provide solutions, and you get the satisfaction of seeing that concern and frustration evaporate and seeing a smile come on the client's face.

Part of the work with Carroll was to complete wills and trusts — standard estate-planning work. Estate planning requires a lot of decisions that are not always easy to make. One reason people fail to do some of these things is that advisors are not patient enough to take their clients through the decision-making process. Often advisors will just say, "Here's the information; make a decision; we'll sign the documents and this will be done." But my approach is: "Here's how these trusts and these estate plans are set up. This is how these documents work. This is the role of the trustee and the executor. Here are the characteristics of the individuals we would like to see in those roles. Either your wife or your husband has those characteristics or they don't. So we'll talk about them. I'll explain how this estate plan works, then later we'll have another meeting to answer your questions, after you have thought about it."

These in-depth conversations bring up issues like, "I don't trust my son with my estate." Or, "I don't think my daughter can run this business." Or, "My wife, God love her, doesn't have the ability to do these things." I ask the client to make "gut checks" to avoid potential disaster. (I have seen these disasters; it is much better, much easier to avoid them than to get out of them.) The estate-planning process is educational, emotional, and almost always takes a number of weeks or months to complete.

We did that with Carroll. He and Gloria drove up from Hot Springs to a large law firm in Little Rock to execute those documents. A few weeks later they were going on a trip to Epcot Center and were anxious to get everything signed. I've made it a practice since then to be there for the signing, but I was not there then.

A few weeks later, I went to Boston for an educational seminar and then on to White Plains for a meeting. From there I called my office to check my messages, and was told, "We have really bad news. Carroll Plumlee died of a heart attack yesterday."

I was just stunned. They had left for Epcot about the same time I had left for my trip. They were traveling with two other couples they knew from their church. Carroll had been driving a motor home, and they had stopped in Tallahassee to service it and eat dinner. The group went into the restaurant, but Carroll was not feeling well—a bad case of indigestion, he thought. He and Gloria went out to the motor home. Within a few minutes he felt worse and slumped over on the bed. Gloria ran into the restaurant to get the other couples: one person was a doctor and another knew CPR. They worked with him until the ambulance arrived. On the way to the Tallahassee Medical Center, the medics worked hard to save his life, but Carroll was pronounced dead on arrival. He was fifty-three years old.

I cut my trip short and returned home immediately. I had mixed emotions. I was glad we had worked hard to develop a good estate plan; Carroll had been at peace about that. He was on track to bring in a new partner or sell his business. He wanted to reduce his workload to have more time for travelling and fishing. It wasn't long before Gloria would be able to retire, after teaching school for thirty years. He had been really upbeat. But I felt tremendous sadness because his life was cut short. I held up very well until the middle of the funeral, but then I just lost it completely. I wept hard for the rest of the ceremony and at the graveside.

I called Gloria as soon as I got back and told her that today was not the day to talk about things, but that I was there to do whatever she needed me to do. She said, "I know I am going to need your help." I told her I would call her in the next couple of days. I said, "You don't need to do anything for the next few days." And she said, "I won't."

The next week I drove to their house, where I had been many times. Gloria, her son, Mike, and I sat down at the dining room table and reviewed the will, and she didn't even remember we had done all this work. It had only been a couple of weeks since we had made the decisions, but she couldn't remember what we had planned. She was at a complete loss as to what was supposed to happen.

This really drove home to me that first-time widows don't have any experience at settling estates. She didn't know what the first step should be. "What do I do now?" she asked me.

The only thing that absolutely has to be done

When I met Sharon the first time, in June of 1997, she had been referred to me by an attorney with whom I had done some work. I'm not sure how I got the information that she was a widow. But my initial reaction was that her situation wasn't really any different from that of any other widow I had worked with.

While we talked in my office, I sensed that she was still struggling with this event in her life. I was silently guessing she had been a widow for a few weeks. When she told me that she had been a widow for three years, I almost fell out of my chair. She had been struggling with her circumstances for nearly three years!

Our meeting lasted a couple of hours. I distinctly remember saying to my staff when she left, "I hope she calls me back because I know I can help her a lot, and I am very concerned about her situation." I had been through the process with other widows, and I felt Sharon wasn't where she was supposed to be at this point. It was very disturbing to me that someone so intelligent was, after three years, still so confused.

Her life had taken her from one immediate and demanding concern to another, beginning with the moment her husband passed away. After the funeral, it was the wedding, then the house, and then running for public office. In her case it took years to get to that moment when she said to herself, "I have to face all these financial matters now." Sharon had managed to delay this reality for nearly three years. For some, that moment comes in only weeks or months.

Imagine, if you will, the frustrations and pressure of needing to make decisions in areas in which you are unfamiliar. Relatives and friends usually don't understand why widows are not able to just go ahead and make those decisions. But until you've experienced this, it's difficult to understand what is going on in the mind of a widow.

Parents, children, siblings, friends are almost always too emotionally involved to understand the impact making decisions has on the widow or widower. However well-meaning they may be, most family and friends can't realize what a huge step forward it is for the widow to become able to make these seemingly small financial decisions.

It is important to understand that it is *not absolutely necessary* to make decisions immediately. The only critical thing that has to be done is to select someone to complete the estate tax return, a report to the federal government that identifies how much property the person owned. That process involves a tax attorney or accountant getting an inventory of all the assets and liabilities owned solely by the decedent. The estate tax form is completed, signed by the executor and tax attorney or accountant, and submitted to the Internal Revenue Service. Within nine months of the date of death, the estate tax return *must* be either filed or extended with the tax paid. That is a decision the survivor is compelled to make.

Other decisions can wait. Maybe they *shouldn't* always wait, but they can be postponed until you get organized enough to make proper decisions. It is *better* to wait than to make hasty decisions.

Usually there is no shortage of people giving advice. Some of them are qualified to be giving advice, and some are not. Some of them may have an agenda. For example, they may have a relative who is a trust officer or stockbroker or an insurance agent who would want very much to sell you something. When your assets are liquid—for example, when you have received the insurance death benefit, when you have the most cash—that moment requires a decision: "What is the best use for this money at the moment?" There are a lot of opportunities during this period of time to take the wrong step or make a wrong decision.

There is an exception to the "only thing that absolutely has to be done" rule. If the ownership of a business or farm is involved, certain actions may have to be taken immediately. These actions are usually very important because a business generally represents a large portion of the assets available to the widow. If so, her objective becomes to get the most money she can in exchange for the business interest. Consequently, making proper business decisions in a timely manner is essential.

If the business is not a corporation or a partnership—that is, if the business is a sole proprietorship—then the executor has to step in and either continue or liquidate, whichever may be in the best interest of the beneficiary of the estate. There is no legal authority for any person to continue that business without a court order. It must be liquidated in the absence of a written agreement to do otherwise.

In the case of a partnership, in the absence of a written agreement, the surviving partner becomes a liquidating partner. The partner has no legal authority without preplanning to continue the business. He or she is obligated to liquidate the business and distribute the assets to the estate according to the partnership ownership. If a written agreement exists, it will dictate the terms by which the partnership is handled.

On the other hand, a corporation has perpetual life, and a limited liability company has continuity of existence. They exist on their own. Those two types of companies continue to exist and have express authority to continue. Sharon has referred to John and "his partner," but they weren't really partners. Technically they were shareholders and officers in a corporation. If either or both of them passed away, the corporation continued to exist. In the absence of an agreement indicating otherwise, the shares of the company were transferred to someone, according to the last will and testament of the deceased shareholder—and almost always the wife inherits the shares. In those circumstances, the widow is suddenly a shareholder in the corporation where her husband used to be the shareholder. She has now inherited his rights of ownership. Not as an officer or an employee, but as a shareholder.

So there are very definite business decisions that require immediate attention. Insofar as preplanning, if the decedent's company is a proprietorship or a partnership, he must grant authority for someone to continue that business. There must be a written agreement to continue the operation of that business—to have the authority to hire people to continue to run it—or to have the authority to sell that business. People who have proprietorships or partnerships should work with their attorney. The attorney drafts documents that legally empower survivors to sell or continue the business in the event of the death of a sole proprietor or partner.

Disclaimers

Sometimes disclaimers are appropriate. A good tax attorney or accountant can help you determine if a disclaimer is appropriate for your situation. A disclaimer is a way of rejecting an inheritance. For example, the husband leaves all his property to his wife but she rejects a savings account in the amount of $50,000. The executor would then turn to the heir next in line—usually her child or children—to deliver the savings account because Mom rejected the inheritance.

Why would this be done? The primary objective would be to take advantage of estate tax savings at the time of the second death. If Mom doesn't need the savings account, then she can direct it to the children at the time of the first death. And it won't be taxed at Mom's death because she doesn't own the savings account; the children do. This strategy is used when the estate was not properly planned while everyone was alive. Obviously, many circumstances must fit for this strategy to make sense.

Estate Taxes

Not everyone must pay taxes on the estate tax form, IRS Form 706. If the net value of estate assets is less than $650,000, then no tax is due. This amount increases each year until 2005 when the exempt amount is $1 million. If things have been properly planned, a couple will be able to pass $2 million to their children without incurring taxes. Though it sounds like a large number, you might be surprised. The Form 706 requires you to add everything you own— even the death benefit of your own life insurance and retirement funds. It's a good idea to check where you stand from time to time, so that you can plan ahead.

Somebody's got to
have a foot on dry land

L ike many other widows and widowers, Sharon was confronted with the need to organize her financial life—her investments, savings, insurance. She also had become a shareholder in a corporation and the owner of rental property. She was faced with the decisions surrounding the addition to her house. She needed goals and objectives—a plan—all in the absence of her "decision partner."

Sharon's husband had a lot of roles in her life, but certainly one of them was that he was her decision partner. Some of the decisions were all his; her decision was to accept that. And some of the decisions were all hers, and he made a decision to accept that. Some of their decisions were 80/20, 70/30, 50/50. But all the decisions were shared in some manner, and there was reliance on a partner—a decision partner.

It's an all-too-common mistake to approach a widow with the attitude of "This is the decision you should make," or "I'm sure your husband would have wanted you to make this decision," or "In my judgment you have all you need for now." It's a mistake to approach a widow with the intent of having her make the decision you think she should make. It's *her* decision. The widow and advisor should become decision partners. A decision partner is a reliable, trustworthy, and *objective* advisor.

I am not trying to fill any void in Sharon's life other than serving as her decision partner. I think there is a big difference. Other people may have tried to be something other than decision partners: "I'm doing this because of our friendship," or "I'm helping because I feel sorry for you." These are statements that should raise red flags.

It's important to understand the emotions of all the parties involved. The widow, of course, struggles with grief and confusion. Family members and friends are grieving as well, but for some reason they often feel they should give the widow advice — and that she should take it. So they may use emotions to influence the widow.

In the midst of all this, there may also be a number of salespersons. A salesperson also uses emotions. A good salesperson is taught to use emotions to sell something. An "advisor" who is using emotion in his or her dialogue is generally a salesperson trying to sell you something. And he or she may be aggressive and persistent in order to do that.

Whether you are a widow or not, one of the most difficult things in working with advisors is to separate sales rhetoric from valuable information. You must be able to make the distinction that some of these advisors are salespeople. Some may have very little product knowledge, very little industry knowledge. But they have been trained and their skills have been honed to precipitate a decision. They know how to close the deal; when the decision is made and a transaction is made, they get paid. It is important to know the difference between a sales pitch and good financial advice. If you are confronted with a sales situation — including over the telephone — ask for information in writing and then get a second opinion. You want to make your decisions based on information.

While he or she certainly must be aware of — and understand — the emotions of the widow, a good advisor avoids involving any emotions in advising the widow and aiding her in decision-making. A good advisor doesn't have to employ any sort of emotional appeal — because a good advisor doesn't have an agenda. In fact, it's a mistake for advisors to use emotions or be emotionally involved because then they get in the same boat the widow's in. Somebody's got to have a foot on dry land.

I don't use emotions when I work with Sharon, or with any of my clients. When we work together, it is a partnering process: I present facts thoroughly and objectively, we review information, and we make decisions. She has never heard me say, "Sharon, you really *ought* to invest in this because John would have wanted it this way." She's never heard me say, "As you have described John, I think he would want you to do this or that." In the time right after their loss, widows are often surrounded by people who are advising them in ways they think their dead husbands would want them advised.

Sharon told me that she had to start telling people, "You're not doing business with John Trusty; you are doing business with me." When Sharon walked into my office, *she* became my client. I am *her* advocate; I take *her* position. I find out what she wants to accomplish, and I determine her level of understanding. Then we adjust to a level where we are making joint decisions as decision partners.

With all my clients, I listen and listen and listen, and then we make decisions together. I simply become a decision partner—so the client relies on me to help make decisions. In turn, I rely on the client to be honest with me that she understands the decisions we are making.

One client of mine has been widowed for some time and has never remarried. Consequently, I continue to be her decision partner in many areas. I've helped my clients buy cars, build homes, buy a telephone and an office building. It's the kind of relationship I have with them. The scope of the work I do goes far beyond designing investment portfolios and making investment decisions. I would guess that half my time is devoted to non-investment issues. Clients don't view me as being strictly in the investment business.

With an objective advisor, what you should feel is "Here is someone who acknowledges me. Here's a person with whom I share mutual respect and with whom I am going to make decisions in a different way." Then you can have confidence you've made the decision because of information, not because of emotions. You've made it together with your decision partner; you've got that reinforcement.

Everybody likes to have reinforcement in making decisions. A widow always needs a good, objective advisor—a decision partner.

Telephone Sales

A good salesperson is taught to use emotions to sell something—even on the telephone. Consumer complaints of investment (and insurance) telephone sales have increased dramatically. In New York alone, complaints have increased 150% in two years. Here are some things to remember, according to Forbes magazine (November 3, 1997):

- *It's impossible for the average investor to "get in on a really good deal";*

- *Any recently issued stock that sells for less than $8 per share will likely have poor performance;*

- *You should work only with companies which have identifiable names. You can call the National Association of Security Dealers (NASD) at 1-800-289-9999 or your state's securities department to check out any company or any salesperson.*

My advice: Use extreme caution about making investments or buying insurance over the telephone. I can't think of a single circumstance where it would be appropriate to buy an investment or insurance from a salesperson over the telephone—ever!

If you don't have confidence in the person, pick up your purse and walk out the door

You can use your intuition and some common-sense questions to find your decision partner. It may not be easy; after all, you've probably never done this before. But asking good questions, making good observations, and relying on your "gut feeling" goes a long way in the process. It is the most important decision you will make. Where do you start?

Your decision partner could be an attorney, or an accountant, or a trust officer, or an insurance agent. Or a financial consultant. It's possible that in one of these professionals, there is a person who will work with you as a decision partner.

It's critical as you identify the proper advisor to be your decision partner that you determine his or her experience and expertise in working with widows. Prospective advisors should be interviewed. You should ask them these questions:

- How many widows do you have among your clientele?
- How many years have you been working with widows?
- Would you have any objections to my calling and asking some of your clients what it is like to work with you?
- How do you get paid?

By interviewing, you can find out if this person is oriented toward working with someone in your situation. Also, these various financial professionals may specialize — working with doctors, or with dentists, or with widows, for example — and they are best equipped, and skilled, and experienced in that area of specialty.

The most important question to ask is: how are you compensated? I think of it as "following the money." For instance, an insurance agent is transaction-oriented. An insurance agent gets paid when a insurance product is sold. A stockbroker is also trans-action-oriented. A stockbroker gets paid when a stock, bond, or mutual fund is bought or sold. You need to understand how the various professionals are compensated. After you've bought the insurance policy, you may discover that the insurance agent doesn't have any more time to spend with you. Or you're not going to do any more investing, so the stockbroker drops out of the picture and works with others.

These professionals can provide valuable services. Just remember what they do and how they get paid.

I had absolute confidence when Sharon walked into my office about what needed to be done, when it needed to be done, and how it needed to be done. When she walked away from that first visit, she said to herself, "There was something different about him than others I've talked to. There's something very different about how he works."

Sharon wasn't involved in the planning process while John was living. She had known her husband's advisors in social situations, but wasn't meaningfully involved in most of the decisions. Then after John died, she was meeting with *his* advisors for the first time as an individual.

Some advisors may still try to work with the dead husband. Who is the client here? I am not suggesting that when a client passes away, his or her survivor would stop using me. I treat my client's spouse as my client. I put both of them on the same plateau. But I don't think you can always assume that a person who has been a good advisor to your husband or to you and your husband will automatically be a good advisor to just you.

Sharon's confrontation with the first contractor she had is an example of this important issue: was this person working with the widow of John Trusty or was he working with Sharon Trusty? The contractor may have been confused about who the client was. This is one of the difficulties in which a widow may find herself when she steps into the middle of a project or business her husband has started. Sharon had had experiences working with other general contractors, and she understood that some people are more difficult to work with than others.

Her construction project also illustrates other decision partner issues. There were certain decisions Sharon had been depending on John for. There were all kinds of things he was going to take care of, and now here she was—flooded with those decisions. At first, she chose to use the general contractor to advise her about how to complete the construction. What happened seems to me a classic case of an advisor trying to take advantage of the situation. Maybe he had ten projects going, all shouting for attention; he may have thought, "I'll just put this *woman* on the back burner. She'll be there. I don't have to worry about her." But he was shocked when she let him go.

My guess is that the second contractor had worked with a woman—possibly a widow—before. And he was more understanding and sympathetic, perhaps because he had also had a death in his family. Sharon said that the first contractor had a very good reputation, but the younger contractor was really the better businessman.

These are important decision-partner issues: gender issues, quality issues.

I think a widow would have a good feel for these issues. I think you would have a gut feeling about an advisor who was condescending to you—and would also have a gut feeling about a person with whom you felt comfortable.

A good advisor is going to put both husband and wife on the same plateau. If you deal with people that way, they have a different response and a different attitude toward you. Whether it's in preplanning or after losing your husband, if you don't have confidence in the person you are working with, pick up your purse and walk out the door.

Let that person go. Go to someone who will help you understand. It could save you lots of money and even more heartache.

Fear is the absence
of information

Over the years I have worked with many widows. I've helped them and my other clients make decisions. If there's anything I've learned in the past twenty-five years, I've learned that when the client makes informed decisions, there are no regrets. When you have all the elements to make a good, sound decision, you can walk away from that decision feeling calm and comfortable. I believe very strongly that fear is the absence of information.

I have found that if emotion—whether the emotion is fear or sorrow—is used to precipitate or coerce a decision, the client will regret that decision, which will most likely be changed later. Sometimes that change is costly.

I've asked Sharon as many questions as she's asked me. "Well, what do you think about …?" "How did you feel when…?" I try to learn what a client's attitude is toward money and toward risk. It's an open flow of quantitative and qualitative information. What I have cultivated in the past twenty-five years is experience and information—a foot on dry land. What the client has is a very emotional struggle with decisions. The client has goals, needs, wants, all of which must properly match this information. The more information you give the client, the more understanding the client gets, the easier it is to make a decision; and when we make a decision, there are no regrets. Even if the outcome is negative.

For instance, Sharon and I discussed the pros and cons of selling some of her bank stock. I did some research, shared it with her, and asked, "What do you think?" As a result of our evaluation of information, we sold some stock. The next day the stock went up two dollars a share. If we had waited a couple more days, we could have sold it for more, but we didn't regret the decision. We made the best decision we could, given the information we had at the time.

Sharon is discovering that we are making decisions with confidence, and she doesn't regret the outcome—because we have discussed the possible outcomes. She's also learning that she has enough in the long run. A financial loss of any kind is huge if you don't know whether you will have enough in the long run. The fear of not having enough prevents decision-making.

In making financial decisions, investment decisions, or tax decisions, you have to do your homework. You must conduct good research and make decisions based on information. It takes a lot of hard work to do that. It's not that difficult, though, to be very consistent in making good financial decisions if you have done this.

The timeline for the decision-making process belongs to the client, not the advisor. The client decides when it's time for her—it's her money, her consequences, her life. There's a very different environment when you have this mutual respect and when you make decisions on a proper timeline. I don't have any problem working with a client who wants to start making decisions very quickly. But if a client wants to make decisions slowly, I don't have any problem with that either. What is *fast* for some people is *slow* for others.

I want to emphasize that the advisor must move at the pace of the client. If the advisor moves too quickly, then the client simply makes no decisions. Nothing gets accomplished. It reminds me of the story of "The Tortoise and the Hare": advisors should be more like the tortoise when working with a widow. Advisors cause more damage rushing their clients instead of waiting for the client's natural pace of making decisions. We're going to cross the finish line sooner or later.

A good advisor is sensitive to the decision-making skills of the client. For example, Sharon's style is her style. My job is to accept that style and not fight it; to understand her style as a constraint or guideline of how we work together. I have other clients with whom I work in entirely different ways. My clients are very different, all seventy of them. I have to recognize that difference in style.

The art is in the advisor's ability to manage his knowledge and experience within the style and emotional posture of this client. It's better to ask, "What areas do you want to work on first? Do you want to work on your last will and testament? Do you want to work on this business matter? Or do you want to work on insurance today?" We then are able to focus on that particular area and make a decision.

Making financial decisions is tough. And the more there is to deal with—business, rental property, stocks, bonds, mutual funds, retirement accounts—the more complicated it is to make them. Forty years ago there were only several hundred stocks traded in the stock market; now there are thousands. Twenty-five years ago, the mutual funds section of the *Wall Street Journal* fit in a little box. Today it covers several pages of small print. Today we are dealing with a far more complicated financial world and far more complicated tax laws. The wealthiest people are as challenged as the person with limited income. They are faced with the same daunting tasks of making investment and tax decisions. Widowhood compounds an already difficult business.

Investing in Stocks

Making an investment in stocks is a long-term proposition. Not understanding this financial principal prevents many investors from making proper investment decisions.

Here are the simple facts: The stock market responds to the economy: when the economy is expanding, the stock market generally goes up; when the economy is in recession, the stock market goes down. The economy is either in recession, or expansion, or in transition to a recession or expansion. Recessions generally last for twelve to eighteen months; expansions usually last two to five years. Even if you make the wrong decision and make a stock investment at the beginning of a recession, you will likely be satisfied with the results in the long term. Long term means several years. Anyone investing in stocks should expect to let that investment work for them for at least five years.

Why bother with stocks? Over several decades, stocks have returned twelve percent each year on the average. Bonds have returned five to eight percent. So it makes sense to invest part of your assets in stocks—the part that you won't likely need for several years—and part of your assets in bonds. The rate of return (after inflation and taxes) for stocks makes them the best long-term investment. Bonds are the best short-term investment. Certificates of deposit and money market accounts are used as savings and emergency funds.

Interestingly, the investor should focus on the long-term objectives and expected results while the financial world provides short-term reports. For example, we advise an investor to be patient and to remember the long-term expected results when there is a short-term market downturn. Yet financial institutions send monthly account statements and quarterly performance reports that tell you what is happening in the short run. Remember that good investment strategies are for the long run.

Her grief was made harder

It doesn't make any difference how simple or complex an outsider might feel the decisions are, they are all *tremendous* in the mind of the widow. And there are men who, when they lose their wives, go through the same process as a woman. It's not gender specific. A human being—man or woman, husband or wife—is going through a terribly difficult loss and faces a host of decisions in the wake of the loss.

Up to this point I have focused on issues that confront someone who has lost her spouse. In this chapter, I want to address how to avoid these issues—in other words, how to preplan. If a couple does a good job of planning while both are living, virtually all the financial and business issues can be addressed in advance. Even if you are already a widow, or widower—and perhaps dealing with matters that were not well planned—you will find helpful information in this chapter. Some of the ideas discussed here may influence your decisions for your own estate plan, for example. You can avoid making the same mistakes twice.

Like most widows and widowers, Sharon immediately had a lot of decisions she was compelled to make. Is this the right casket? Who will be the pallbearers? Where are people going to sit? And I'm sure there was a lot of second-guessing. Not only was she trying to guess what John's wishes might have been, but children and other immediate family members have their opinions about all these details, too. So even simple decisions become enormous decisions. Sharon was tired because she had to agonize, to struggle with every decision, and every decision, big or little, *seemed* enormous.

The best environment in which to make these decisions is before the event occurs. Sharon has said, "We thought we were very well prepared." But they weren't nearly as well prepared as they could have been. From her point of view now they could have been a lot better prepared concerning business arrangements, investments, and even the funeral. They hadn't planned at all for John's death; they hadn't planned for the decisions Sharon had to face.

Thinking through these events can lead to decisions that dramatically impact the outcome. For example, everyone who signs a last will and testament has named an executor, usually his or her spouse. An executrix is a female executor. The decision to name a spouse as executor or executrix is almost always based on sentiment. Why? You are choosing someone to do a job who has no experience, no qualifications for the job, especially if your estate is complex. Why would you hire someone who has never done this before to complete this very complicated and time-consuming job? It's on-the-job training for one time! It doesn't make sense. The same applies to children who are similarly inexperienced.

Am I suggesting that your spouse should lose control over your estate? Of course not. The better way might be to name co-executors to work together. You could name your spouse as a co-executor with another party, a qualified professional who has experience in these matters. That other party could be an individual or a trust company. In fact, you don't even have to be specific in naming that other party; that other party could be chosen at the time of your death by your spouse and/or your children. Family members remain in control, but a qualified professional does all the work while your spouse is grieving.

I prefer for the client to be more specific when determining a co-trustee/executor. For example, you could name a specific person or specific criteria for selecting that person. Moreover, this issue should be revisited regularly by the couple. The answer will likely change from one year to the next as confidants, experience, and circumstances change.

If all of this is well planned, this is what happens when your death occurs: your spouse chooses a co-executor who tends to financial matters. If the co-executor is an institution, she has the flexibility to change institutions. If the co-executor is a person, she has the power to replace that person. In other words, she makes one decision and chooses the most appropriate party at the most appropriate time.

The next step is the trust. It is important to understand trusts, and my objective here is to provide only the basics. A complete discussion of trusts could fill volumes. If you want more information on trusts, see the reference list at the end of this book for suggested reading.

There are two basic types of trusts. One is established while you are living (an *inter vivos* trust, or living trust), while the other is set up at your death (a testamentary trust). The living trust is set up — usually by both spouses — during their lifetimes, with both spouses named as trustees. They then transfer all their assets to the trust. It works best to transfer everything you own, even your home, to the trust. The trust assets are used for the couple's benefit only. At the time of the first death, the trust assets are used for the benefit of the surviving spouse. At the death of the surviving spouse, the trust assets are passed to the heirs. One of the advantages of a living trust is the avoidance of probate. Remember that probate retitles property at death to your heirs. If a living trust is used effectively, you and your spouse do not own property, your trust owns all your property. Since you are the trustee, you control all the trust assets, and the trust assets must be used to benefit you. So there is little practical difference in owning assets in a living trust and owning the assets outright. Every widow should consider establishing a living trust — because it avoids probate.

The other type of trust, the testamentary trust, works basically the same way, but there is an important difference. The trust lies within your last will and testament and is not established until you die. Therefore when you pass away, your executor sets up the trust according to your will, probates the estate for the authority to transfer your assets to the trust, then turns the assets over to the trustee. A testamentary trust — a trust inside your will — does not avoid the time and expense of probate.

A trust provides certain protections for your family and appoints a trustee to manage the assets for their benefit. A trustee is a fiduciary. A trustee must meet the highest standards of conduct. A trustee is held to the highest professional standards in making all financial decisions in the best interest of the beneficiary. (For more discussion on trustees as fiduciaries, see "The highest standards of conduct," page 125.)

The trustee has an awesome responsibility because he or she makes a lot of decisions. In creating a trust, just as in writing a will, there's a dilemma: is your spouse qualified to be a good trustee? If not, name your spouse as co-trustee with the power to name the co-trustee. It works the same as the co-executor arrangement I've discussed above. All the complicated financial, tax, investment and business decisions are dealt with by the co-trustees. But, again, the survivor makes one primary decision: who is the best co-trustee for me at this time?

With a will, the role of the executor is only to retitle the property that was owned solely by the decedent. John's will provided, essentially, that if something happened to him, everything would go to Sharon. Nothing the two of them owned jointly was probated because it passed automatically to the survivor. But everything titled in John's name only had to be probated. So the probate process, which typically takes several months, serves only to get a court order to retitle solely owned property from the decedent to the heirs. Then you must file documents to change the title to all the property. Once the property is transferred from the estate to the heirs, the role of the executor ends.

If a trust is created in the will, the co-executors would transfer the property to a trust. A trust stays intact almost always for the life of the surviving spouse and sometimes even for the lives of the children. A trust is very long-term, and many changes can occur over time. Therefore, the design of a trust is extremely important and should be well thought through.

It would have been easier for Sharon had she had a co-executor to come in and say, "OK, you and I are co-executors. Here is the list of what we have to do. These are the steps. As I take you through the steps, you ask any questions that you want." There would have been a clear course of action — in writing. And Sharon and her co-executor would have completed this process as a team. That would have been much easier than Sharon's being out there by herself dealing with all these tasks — tasks with which she had no experience.

The proper way is for a couple to sit down with their advisor and think all of this through. If I had been sitting at the kitchen table with John and Sharon Trusty, we would have had these questions:

* How good is each of you at making these decisions?
* What are your *strong points*?
* What are your *weak points*?
* Is it appropriate to use a co-trustee?
* If you use a co-trustee, who is that person?
* What if you become disenchanted with him or her? How do you fire that person and find an appropriate replacement?
* Who is that person specifically?
* What are his or her credentials?
* What does that other party (the co-trustee) bring to the table as far as skill and experience at keeping things organized, keeping things businesslike, and getting the job done?
* How are the heirs involved?

If the advisor is doing a good job, it's really amazing how the couple will answer honestly: "She's really not good in these areas." Or "He's really not very good in those areas." Most people, regardless of gender, do not feel comfortable making decisions all alone about taxes, investments, and other financial questions. They shouldn't. These are very complex issues that require focus and constant attention. Many successful, well-educated people are experts in certain areas, but they're not necessarily experts in finances.

Working with the advisor, you begin to put together a plan that really works. You determine whether the co-trustee might be a bank trust department, a family member, or a financial professional. It will vary from one family to another.

As with many widows and widowers, Sharon's pain and confusion were compounded: she was grieving over her loss and at the same time struggling with understanding decisions about her finances. Her grief was made harder.

In my experience with other clients, I've found it can take *years* to come to grips with these financial issues: to learn your financial choices and responsibilities and to get comfortable with them. Sharon has a complex set of circumstances; her challenges are daunting. But it can take a lot of time even when the estate is fairly simple.

I have in my office a list of famous people who did an extremely poor job of planning their estates. That list includes some of the most famous accountants — men — and attorneys and show business people in the United States. Just because you work, or just because you are an accountant, or an attorney, or whatever you are, it doesn't mean you have cultivated the proper skills and have done the proper planning to be a good executor or trustee.

A Letter of Intent

People resist planning and decision-making for death and retirement.

People avoid getting down to doing specific retirement planning because of the fear of coming up short. If you are 55 years old, and you add everything up and run a computer program that tells you you need lots more money than you had thought, well, that's depressing. That's not really a happy thing to have to sit down and deal with. So people tend to put off doing it.

To sit down and plan for a funeral, to plan the steps that somebody would take in the event of your death is not particularly appealing either. Sitting down as a couple and saying, "OK, let's suppose that one of us dies. What funeral arrangements do you want? How are we going to deal with the decisions?"

I like the idea of a "letter of intent." The concept may originate from the kind of instructions, or directions if you will, often written by parents of children with special needs, instructions describing how they wish decisions to be made for their child. But anyone can have a letter of intent.

Now imagine if a husband and wife were able to write a letter of intent—maybe even involve somebody from the funeral home. Instructions would be recorded about the casket, the flowers, the music, and many other details. If you write and sign a letter of intent, your survivor simply follows it. If other family members want to discuss these matters, the survivor can show them the letter of intent and simply say, "This is how he wanted things to be. All the decisions have been made." You can relieve your loved ones of a huge amount of stress and decision-making.

I feel very strongly about the letter of intent, a document that addresses how you want these decisions that surround your death to be handled. It is another way of taking a burden off your loved ones.

A Written Employment Agreement

Sharon didn't have a document that explained John's salary arrangement with his company. There was no clear understanding how long John's salary would be conferred to her after his death. Had John become disabled, my guess is his salary would have continued for a period of time. As it was, in the absence of a written agreement, it stopped at his death. The company couldn't continue to pay his salary indefinitely, and Sharon couldn't expect to receive his salary indefinitely. She didn't know what to expect because of the lack of a written agreement.

In the absence of a written agreement, there is often a verbal agreement or understanding. Verbal agreements are simply unacceptable. *The standard of practice is that you have a written agreement. It doesn't do to be sitting around with your business partner and say, "Let's not talk about such a horrible event as your death. But if you pass away first, I'll take care of your wife, and if I die first, you take care of my wife." What does "take care of" mean?*

Women should sit their husbands down and say, "Tell me what your understanding is with the business if you should die. Is there an understanding that your salary will continue for a period of time? Will the company or another owner buy our interest in the business? If so, are the arrangements in writing? Let's read the written agreement together so that I can understand."

With all our clients we go through this process, so everyone clearly understands. We put it in writing. Everybody signs it. There's no guesswork. These written agreements essentially become financial instruments—as important as a life insurance policy.

You walk in and see
a nice foyer...and you
may be intimidated

People usually need the services of professionals from a handful of disciplines—the accountant, the attorney, the banker, the bank trust officer (which I'll discuss in the next chapter), the insurance agent, the stockbroker, perhaps the real estate agent. But widows, like most other people, may not understand how to work effectively with the practitioners—the professionals—in those various disciplines.

There are two important considerations in choosing these professionals. The first is the person's qualifications. The second is understanding how the person is paid.

Too often people make the mistake of engaging the services of a professional without asking questions about his or her qualifications. Even in deciding to use a new doctor, for instance, a lot of people simply ask co-workers or friends to recommend one without checking his or her qualifications.

People are often intimidated by people in these professions. Yes, even socially and financially successful people can be intimidated by walking into a law office, for example. You walk into an office on the thirty-seventh floor and see a nice foyer, wood paneling, Oriental rugs, and you may be intimidated. You shouldn't be. After all, *you're* the client, and you're paying the bill.

I advise people when they go to see these professionals not to be intimidated but rather to ask these basic questions:

- How long have you been in this line of work?
- What are your credentials?
- How have you kept up-to-date?
- What are we going to do here? What will be the scope of our work?
- How much will this cost?

That process—asking an attorney or another professional questions, especially "How much are you going to charge me?"—is foreign to many people. You don't need to be intimidated by any environment or any profession. In fact, if you have a series of questions—simple, direct, clear questions—it establishes two important things: it indicates to the professional that you are somewhat knowledgeable and will expect him or her to be accountable; and it gives you a sense of control. Such an approach can increase your confidence in the presence of an "expert." It will help you realize the expert is a servant and is accountable to you. The key is to *ask questions.* You cannot ask too many questions. You learn by asking questions. When you learn, you understand. And when you understand, you have more confidence and less fear.

It doesn't make sense to go to your optometrist to get a tooth pulled. But that's what people sometimes do when they work with advisors. For example, people will meet with an accountant and assume the accountant can give them tax advice *and* investment advice *and* even legal advice. Moreover, they assume that since the professional is knowledgeable, skilled, and experienced, then he or she must be skilled in all areas. Consequently, many people accept an insurance agent's or stockbroker's assurances—"We can help you with that trust," or "We can help you settle your estate"—only to discover he or she was interested in making a sale. After the sale has been made, the discussion is likely to end.

Your insurance agent or stockbroker usually isn't qualified to advise you about your estate plan. All the professionals mentioned above have their own areas of expertise. Even within those areas, there are specialties. For instance, an insurance agent might sell automobile and homeowner's insurance while another agent might sell surety bonds to builders. They are both insurance agents, yet they have their own specialties. The same applies to attorneys, accountants—all the financial disciplines. It is unlikely that you will need all these professionals at the same time. On the other hand, our world has become very complex and you will need most of them at least once. Just make sure you "qualify" them and that they give you advice within their specialty. Don't go to your optometrist to get your molar filled.

As you work with these experts, interview them to learn their qualifications and follow the money.

An *accountant* is trained to create a set of books, to prepare tax returns, and to discuss tax-saving strategies, each of these being a specialty. Many accountants are able to discuss tax strategies and other planning issues in addition to keeping books and preparing tax returns. But the vast majority have not been trained to offer investment advice or sell insurance, or make real estate or banking transactions. They have, of course, been attendant to some of these transactions; they have observed them and been involved in them. But their core training has prepared them to do the things they get paid to do — keep books and file tax returns.

An *attorney* is trained to prepare legal documents and handle litigation. A tax attorney does basic legal work but focuses on estate and retirement planning. Attorneys are not trained to give investment advice or prepare tax returns. When you realize that someday you are going to pass away and you want your estate to pass to your heirs, you go to an attorney; the attorney drafts the legal documents for you. You realize that you want your business partner to be able to run your company without restrictions; the attorney prepares that document. Attorneys draft legal documents and take legal actions as necessary to solve problems for clients. They don't do banking, investments, tax returns, or real estate selling.

Attorneys and accountants are compensated with either an hourly fee or a flat fee. Before you use their services, while you are defining the scope of the work, you should ask how much it is going to cost. There is nothing wrong with asking, "We are asking you to draft these documents. How much will we have to pay you?" It's as simple and straightforward as that. Don't be shy about asking accountants and attorneys to tell you how much they will charge for their work. If they know what they're doing, they can give you at least a range of the cost involved.

A *banker* makes loans. He doesn't charge a fee. You can talk to him until you are blue in the face, and he won't charge you any money. Bank officers are not trained to keep books or give tax advice, to give legal or investment advice, or to sell insurance. They are trained to set up bank accounts, make loans, and manage cash. They don't get paid anything directly from dealing with you. Instead the bank charges you fees for the services it provides, and interest on the money it lends you.

The role of the *bank trust officer*, however, is radically different. I will take up the role of the bank trust officer in detail in the next chapter.

The *insurance agent* is trained to understand insurance products and how they fit an individual's needs. The *stockbroker* is trained to gather enough information about clients and investments to make a good fit. The *real estate agent* is trained to understand real estate transactions and to make transactions on behalf of his or her clients.

Remember: Insurance agents, stockbrokers, and real estate agents spend a great deal of time developing sales skills and sales rhetoric to precipitate a decision.

Also remember an insurance agent makes a commission from the transaction of an insurance sale and a stockbroker makes a commission on investment transactions. When an insurance agent, or stockbroker, or real estate agent tells you he is going to make retirement planning and retirement projections and help with setting up your estate, you need to remind yourself that these professionals don't get paid for this kind of work. Put yourself in their shoes: would you spend a lot of time giving out free advice that doesn't pertain to your particular area of specialty or qualification?

And how reliable is that advice? Why would you expect that advice to be reliable? The general rule is *caveat emptor*—let the buyer beware. The consumer has a responsibility to be aware of the differences between salespersons and other advisors. This responsibility makes it even more important to understand the specific roles of the various financial professionals.

I don't mean to create the impression that all salespeople are heartless or uncaring. They deliver valuable services. Many times, in fact, they motivate the client to begin the planning process. Often getting a second opinion to a sales offer can lead the client to serious decisions—which can lead to constructive planning.

The reality of working with salespersons is *transactions with commissions*. I don't have any problem with a person making a living from commission sales; I have done it myself. But no harm can come from their discussing their commissions before the sale is made. Ask them to do so.

Each of these financial disciplines is regulated by laws that dictate the behavior of professionals within them. And almost all of these professionals are members of professional organizations that prescribe basic practice standards. These practice standards always include a system or procedure for removing or disciplining members who don't follow the rules. An attorney can be disbarred by the American Bar Association. An accountant can lose his standing with the American Institute of Certified Public Accountants. An insurance agent can lose his license to sell insurance. A stockbroker can be censured, fined, or lose his license to sell investments. You need to know that there is recourse when these professionals don't follow their professional rules.

There is also recourse when damage is done. Many people mistakenly think they have no recourse if a professional has acted inappropriately and caused damage, in the form of lost value, potential value, or lost money. There are clear, distinct steps you can follow to get redress. The first step is to contact your state attorney general's office. The attorney general's office can direct you to the appropriate governmental agency or professional organization.

I have seen some people who suffered significant financial loss unwilling to seek redress. If it happened to you, then it may happen to someone else in the future. It takes only one person to step up and ask for a review. If you have been wronged, you have nothing to lose by coming forward. After all, that's why these procedures for recourse were established.

We are in the beginning of what may prove to be a sea change in the financial world. Laws are being changed in several states to permit accountants to sell investments and make commissions. Banks are now permitted to sell insurance products, and their affiliates now sell investments. I expect this trend to continue.

Stockbrokers don't call themselves stockbrokers. They refer to themselves as "financial advisors" or "financial consultants." But they are still the same: they sell investments for a commission. It hasn't been many years since attorneys were forbidden to advertise. They could do nothing more than put their name and number in the telephone book. Now look in the yellow pages under ATTORNEYS. We don't know what kinds of changes are going to happen next in the legal field.

There is discussion in Washington now about changing the basic laws that govern banks, insurance companies, and investment companies. The result could be a blurring in the functions these institutions are permitted by law to perform. It will be even more important that you be able to get disclosure as to what a professional's qualifications are, what the cost of the service will be, and how the person is going to get paid. There will always be traditional professional service providers in each one of these disciplines, but it may become more difficult to find them.

What is a
Certified Financial Planner Licensee?

Not every person who is described as a financial planner holds the Certified Financial Planner designation. To earn the CFP mark, individuals must meet the continuing education, ethics, examination and experience prerequisites set by the Certified Financial Planner Board of Standards, Inc.—the professional regulatory body. CFP candidates must study and successfully complete a demanding examination process, administered by the CFP Board, covering 106 topics in six disciplines: asset management, employee benefits, estate planning, insurance, investments, and retirement. Additionally, individuals must meet continuing education, ethics, and work experience criteria.

The highest standards of conduct

Other than an independent, fee-only advisor, the bank trust officer has the most potential to provide very good overall financial advice. However there are a number of considerations in selecting a bank trust officer.

A bank trust officer is a *fiduciary*. There is no higher standard of professional conduct than that of a fiduciary. *The American Heritage Dictionary* defines a fiduciary as "one who holds something in trust for another... a person who stands in a special relation of trust, confidence, or responsibility in his obligation to others ... " Court cases and legal opinions over many years have expanded the definition. In the 1830 court case of *Harvard College v Armory*, the duty owed by a trustee to beneficiaries was described:

> All that can be required of a trustee to invest is, that he shall conduct himself faithfully and exercise sound discretion. He is to observe how men of prudence, discretion, and intelligence manage their own affairs, not in regard to speculation, but in regard to the permanent disposition of their funds, considering the probable income, as well as the probable safety of capital to be invested.

It is because of the long-standing view of a fiduciary that many husbands name banks as the trustee for their spouse. Bank trust officers handle all the financial affairs for the spouse who is the beneficiary of the trust. They will see to it that trust assets are held properly and in safekeeping, that all dividends and interest are properly credited to the client's account; they will pay the monthly bills, pay property taxes—do everything a "prudent" person should do. In theory, a bank trust officer can be a good decision partner. But just as in all other financial matters, you must check qualifications and follow the money.

A bank trust department is registered with the same agency in each state as is a bank. State regulations generally require two registrations, since the bank and the trust department are two different entities. They have different objectives and purposes.

The bank is regulated by the Comptroller of the Currency, which is part of the Federal Reserve Bank. Banks must follow specific rules and procedures relating to bank deposit and loan procedures. The trust department, however, provides a service for a fee and is guided by an entirely different set of rules. These rules, which are mostly legal requirements governing how a trustee must behave with assets held in trust, have been created and shaped by laws and court cases.

Bank trust departments charge a percentage fee — generally one percent of the account balance — to manage assets. Larger accounts may be charged lower fees. The fact that bank trust departments are paid with fees means that you should expect objective, competent decisions in the handling of your financial affairs. Bank trust officers aren't transaction-oriented; they don't earn commissions. They have the duty to manage your funds as well as possible.

Many people name banks as trustees for their estates because out of habit, attorneys suggest it. They usually do this because they presume their spouse is not capable of making good financial decisions. At the time a death occurs, all the estate assets are swept into the bank trust department and the trustee decides where to put all those assets. Many times the trustee will put some of those assets in its affiliated bank or investment company. In some cases, that is appropriate; in others, it is more appropriate for the assets to go elsewhere. For example, some trustees will invest in mutual funds that are manufactured by the bank. Never mind that there are more than ten thousand mutual funds in the marketplace. Never mind that many of those mutual funds outperform the bank's mutual fund. Such are the vagaries of using bank trust departments. Sometimes they are not completely objective.

In the past, the bank trust officer's investment decisions were guided by the Prudent Man Rule. The Prudent Man Rule stated that a trustee must make all decisions for their beneficiary consistent with the decisions that a prudent man with experience, education, and skill would make. This led to "legal lists"—a list of universally acceptable investments—that trust officers came to rely upon. These legal lists contain many financial instruments offered by banks. In recent decades, this lack of objectivity has led to the Third Restatement of Trusts, a body of regulations in the process of being adopted by each state. The Third Restatement dictates how trustees should invest assets; how they should execute investment transactions; how they should diversify the portfolio; and other technical information affecting standard of care required by a trustee. The Third Restatement of Trusts simply modernizes the Prudent Man Rule and legal lists. The latter two will soon be a thing of the past as all states adopt the Third Restatement of Trusts.

The trustee in the bank trust department has the highest legal obligation to act in a fiduciary capacity on behalf of the beneficiaries of a trust. A fiduciary accepts full and personal responsibility for all actions taken in his or her capacity. Trustees are held to the highest standards of conduct in the financial world. Many bank trust departments have thousands of clients but—surprisingly—only maybe a few trust officers. It is not uncommon for a trust officer to have to deal with *hundreds of accounts* of all sizes. The procedures and methods as to how the trustee assesses the needs, tolerance for risk, and cash flow for each of those clients vary dramatically from one bank to another. Often the treatment of clients becomes mechanical. Perhaps understandably, trust officers end up making across-the-board decisions, decisions that affect all the accounts they manage regardless of the specific objectives of the beneficiary. Therefore the portfolios may be structured in a very general sense and not tailored to each client's particular and individual needs. A bank trust officer simply can't get around to seeing a few hundred people in a proper way.

In a trust situation, you should ask these questions of the trust officer:

- How long have you been employed by this trust department?
- How long have you been in the trust business?
- What are your qualifications?
- How many portfolios are you currently managing?
- Are your portfolios designed and monitored by you or someone else?
- Does my portfolio look like all the other accounts you have?
- What methods do you employ to make my portfolio fit my needs?
- Are there any conflicts of interest?
- Does this bank manufacture financial products which are sold to the trust accounts?

Bank trust officers don't get paid large salaries, and there tends to be a large turnover among them. Many times a trust officer goes to work for a bank, gets assigned a large number of clients, gets a better offer from another institution, and moves on. It is unusual to meet a trust officer who has been with the same bank for a long time. When a trust officer leaves, a new officer is assigned to your trust account. Then the entire "getting acquainted" process begins over again. Rarely will the new trust officer do a comprehensive review—he doesn't have time. I have talked to some people who have had over a half-dozen trust officers.

People will set up trusts through their wills naming a bank as their trustee and leaving their spouse and children with that bank as trustee for the rest of their lives. That is because the last will and testament provides for a specifically named institution ("The XYZ State Bank and Trust"). To change a bank trustee once it is legally established by death creates a real legal problem.

Another problem with naming a specific bank trustee is that people may move. Once I was working with a client who had a trust account in Indiana. We reviewed the performance of the bank trust department and it wasn't good. The client asked the bank to transfer the trust to an Arkansas bank since they had moved here, but the bank refused. The bank trust department maintained that they would not be removed because the trust in the will was irrevocable. Consequently this family found themselves living in a state different than that of the trustee, who was providing poor performance. They were stuck. This is avoided by planning so that the spouse names the co-trustee, as I discussed in an earlier chapter.

With all the recent bank mergers, many concerns have developed. One of my biggest concerns is that bank trustees have a duty and obligation to put their client's needs before their own interests. The bank trust officer should look at the entire investment world: now nearly ten thousand mutual funds; thousands of bonds; thousands and thousands of stocks. In this vast investment world, the trustee has the obligation to act in the best interest of his trust beneficiaries. But now very large banks are creating and selling investment products like mutual funds. And so the bank trust officer is often confronted with a dilemma: "Look, I have these mutual funds that are manufactured by the bank. Or I can choose from the entire universe of mutual funds. Which should I choose?" So the trust officer may buy the bank's mutual funds—regardless of their performance. With very large banks, there may be essentially three companies: the bank, the trust department, and now the investment department, manufacturing investment products they sell to anyone but also sell to the trust department. That creates a potential conflict of interest.

Now banks also sell insurance products. You should ask your trust officer if any of the trust accounts contain investment or insurance products made or sold by the bank. You should ask:

• What conflicts of interest exist?
• Does this bank manufacture investment or insurance products?
• Are any of those products being put into the accounts you manage?
• How does the bank deal with those issues?

If you follow the money on this, the bank is making one percent or more on the money that is in the trust, but they may also be making another one to one-and-a-half percent on the mutual funds—and more on insurance products—they buy to put in the trust. I don't always have a problem with this if the mutual funds the trust department is buying for its clients have superior performance. But when they have inferior performance, a clear conflict of interest exists. It is not in keeping with The Third

Restatement of Trusts, the Prudent Man Rule, or the acceptable standard of care required of trustees.

Conflict of Interest

From your point of view, conflict of interest simply means that your interest comes before all others. Another way to look at it is from the trustee's point of view, in which case conflict of interest means the client's interests come before all other interests.

The financial consultant
should be a relationship manager

To successfully manage financial decisions, you need to be able to recognize when you are working with a capable financial professional — whether an accountant, attorney, banker, trust officer, insurance agent, stockbroker, or real estate agent. This may be quite difficult to do.

A financial consultant works with these various professionals on behalf of his or her client — at the appropriate time and with the appropriate information. In my work, I look for a good fit between a client and qualified professionals. Further, we discuss the scope of the work to be done and what the cost will be. I've found a variety of skills, abilities, and experiences among the different professional firms with which we work. I work with various professionals in concert to meet the needs of each client. It's essentially the proper management of professional relationships — acting as a relationship manager.

Clients often lack either experience or knowledge in working with these professionals and are not typically skillful at orchestrating them. Everybody has to be kept informed. In order to do a good job, an accountant needs certain information; an attorney needs different information. It's extremely important for a financial consultant to have the experience, skill, and respect of other professionals to advise the client appropriately in each one of those disciplines. That requires a lot of work and knowledge, if not art.

In the 1980s I started referring to myself as a *financial consultant* instead of a financial planner. I viewed financial *planning* as gathering qualitative and quantitative information from a client, writing a plan, and discussing with clients appropriate financial decisions. Financial *consulting* involves much more proactive financial decision-making. Consulting is much more focused on implementation rather than on writing plans. Financial plans can actually be written by an accountant or stockbroker or attorney or even a computer. Back in the 1980s, various disciplines were in fact writing financial plans. It was a basic process of providing a written plan to the client, who would decide whether to accept or reject the advice. The implementation was very much up to the client.

As a result, financial planning was no longer taken seriously on Wall Street — *Forbes* magazine ran a cover with a monkey and the caption, "Is this your financial planner?"—because insurance agents and stockbrokers called themselves "financial planners"; it helped them close sales without the client's realizing it. This left clients very dissatisfied because they thought they were getting broad-based, objective financial planning. Instead they were being sold a product.

A financial plan is basically a snapshot of the client's financial situation, with recommendations for the current situation. Often a financial plan is constructed by an insurance agent to close an insurance sale or by a stockbroker to result in more investment transactions. More likely than not, if a sales organization contacts you about creating a financial plan, that plan is intended to direct you to a transaction.

When you follow the money, you finally get to the bottom line: the real objective of the financial plan. Ask yourself:

* Is this financial plan prepared by a sales organization?
* Is this person who's advising me acting in my best interest?
* Or are his or her considerations of compensation keeping him or her from being objective?

With all our questions, we are looking for *objectivity* on the part of the advisor. The financial plan may provide accurate information but little appropriate advice. There's a big difference between information and advice. For instance, you could submit your financial information to an investment company and separately to an insurance company, asking both for a financial plan. And you would undoubtedly get completely different recommendations.

Practitioners who work for sales institutions cannot be objective. I'm not sure how anyone can expect them to be. They may be highly qualified to use their line-up of financial products, but they cannot be objective enough to write a good financial plan. Their goal, after all, is the transaction, the sale. They win trips based on how much they sell. They don't win a trip to Hawaii for taking you to an attorney and getting your trust set up. They don't win a Caribbean cruise for sitting down with your accountant and making sure your books are set up properly or for making your cash management more efficient with your bank. Salespersons win trips to exotic places—and they get paid—when you buy stocks, bonds, mutual funds, insurance policies, annuities from them. That is their goal. They don't get service awards. I have never seen a trophy awarded to a stockbroker or insurance agent for serving a client particularly well. They get awards for selling more than the next guy. And that's perfectly OK—as long as you understand that.

The ability to listen is the key

To begin the process of organizing a good financial strategy, the consultant first gathers quantitative and qualitative data on the client. Getting the quantitative data is simple: the consultant reviews financial statements and reports, accountant statements, legal documents, employment agreements, things that are on paper.

The skill, the art is in listening to the client. Listening is how the consultant gathers qualitative information. The ability to listen is the key element for a good financial consultant. It's often more important to know *why* the client bought something rather than *what* he or she bought. I ask a lot of questions. I am trying to determine how and why my client makes decisions.

When Sharon and I had our first meeting, ninety-nine percent of what I did was ask questions and listen. If you ask questions and then listen carefully to the answers, people will usually open up and tell you what you need to hear. Sharon knew I was listening to her *because I was asking good questions.* I knew no benefit would have been derived from talking to Sharon about financial concepts at that first meeting. It was too early. She wasn't yet ready to receive that information. Part of the art of financial consulting is understanding when your client is ready to take that step forward.

It is important that the consultant is focused on each meeting. He or she should ask before each interview, "Do we work on a specific matter today? Or do we talk about more general things?" You have to be sensitive to how your client is feeling that day. Sometimes I prepare for a meeting filled with technical information only to realize that the client is not in the proper frame of mind to make decisions. I recognize the mood, and we will end the meeting without completing my objectives for the meeting.

But that's OK. I've learned that if a client isn't up to making decisions on a certain day, you wait for another day. Patience is the key. The relationship is very businesslike and the environment informed—so that decisions can be made.

In my work I don't ask clients to fill out forms listing financial information and send it off to headquarters for a computer to create a generic report. Several years ago I wrote financial plans that were sixty or seventy pages long. One of my favorite clients drove in from out of town to review his newly prepared financial plan. We started about 8:30 in the morning and finished about 5:00 in the afternoon. At sixty or seventy pages, his plan couldn't have been more thorough. But that was a lot to absorb in one day.

I seldom do that anymore. Over the years I've learned to create financial plans in components. The all-at-once approach is overwhelming to most clients. It is very difficult to review and comprehend so much information. Our work covers all the financial aspects of the client—even better than years ago. But now I present the information in components so that it's more manageable and, ultimately, better implemented.

A distinction of my work is my independence. I don't work for an insurance company or bank or financial organization or any other institution. I work for my clients. My agenda—the agenda of the independent financial consultant—is to help clients make wise decisions about managing assets. That's what I'm paid to do. I have the attitude that I am a fiduciary for my clients—an informal trustee, if you will.

Once again, you have to follow the money. The method of compensation for financial consultants is important. People generally know the only way to get objective advice is to pay for it. And this most likely means that whether it's a few hundred dollars or a few thousand dollars, you will have to pay for it.

I can remember the moment in 1981 when I first asked someone to pay me a fee. The client had an insurance agent, a good friend who lived next door, from whom he wanted to buy a life insurance policy. I told him I would charge him $300 to look at the insurance proposals and advise him what to do. The idea of a fee — I had always worked on commission — was stressful. I broke out in a sweat. He probably thought that was too much because I didn't hear from him again. But for me, it was an important step.

There is debate in our industry whether we should charge by the hour or by a percentage of assets under management. Some of the work I do is more appropriate for an hourly fee. But for most of my work, I charge a percentage of assets under management. I don't engage a client thinking we are going to have a short-term relationship. Remember, independent financial consultants are not transaction-oriented. My objective is to make my client wealthier by making good decisions. So I think this method of compensation fits my practice well.

Financial consulting is complex; you can't take a snapshot today and expect the picture to stay the same for a long time. *Virtually all the information changes the very next day.* Every one of my clients has issues that have to be addressed all year — important financial issues that have profound, long-term impact. So I think a fair way to price my service is by a percentage of assets under management. If any and every decision I make for my client makes her wealthier, she becomes happier. And if I get a small percentage of that, then I am rewarded for making good financial decisions.

Only a long-term holistic professional relationship is acceptable to me. Regardless of the client's age, I foresee a multigenerational relationship spanning many years. After working with a client for a few years, I simply expect to work with them or their children for the rest of my life. The completeness of the relationship creates certain characteristics of my practice. First, I want to be available to my clients to assist in any decision they need to make. For example, each time a certain widow client is confronted with a financial issue greater than $1,000, she calls me. Sometimes she calls me a lot; sometimes I don't hear from her. But she knows I'm here.

This arrangement limits the number of clients with whom I work. I have discovered that I can maintain only about seventy clients. One person simply cannot provide financial consultation for several hundred people; there is simply not enough time. Consequently, the number of clients a prospective decision partner has should tell you something. If you are trying to select a consultant and you learn he has hundreds of clients, you may conclude that consultant is either transaction-oriented or does not pursue a holistic relationship. For some widows, that may be acceptable; for others, it won't be.

Sometimes a percentage-of-assets method is not the best fee arrangement. Some people simply want an update on their situation. A proper fee arrangement for such a situation is an hourly fee. But I have a concern about such arrangements. Although it saves money, the responsibility is on the individual to come to the consultant asking for the review. It's human nature to procrastinate, especially when it comes to planning for death and retirement. When a consultant is working for a percentage of assets under management, the consultant has the responsibility to take planning issues to the client.

Financial decisions must be followed through: implementation is extremely important. Many financial institutions conduct seminars. These seminars are designed to sell a financial product. Often people will attend a financial seminar where it is recommended they set up a living trust. Living trusts are appropriate estate planning for many family situations. But on closer review we find the presentations are designed to lead to the sale of some kind of financial product for a commission. Evidently these seminars result in sales; otherwise these salespersons would give up seminars and sell their products in other ways. But not every planning strategy is appropriate for every family. Many factors that make a strategy appropriate for you may make the same strategy inappropriate for the person sitting next to you. Therefore the strategy or solution the seminar offers may or may not be appropriate for the situation.

Even when it is appropriate, often the strategy is not properly implemented. Using the living trust as an example, your assets must be transferred to the trust for the strategy to work properly. One of the primary objectives of a living trust is to avoid the time and expense of probate. The deeds on real property must be signed over to the trust and filed with the office of the county clerk. Beneficiary arrangements in life insurance policies and retirement plans must be coordinated with the trust. Therefore there may be a trust in place, but it is ineffective to avoid probate because it holds no assets. To make all of this even more confusing, it is not best in every case to transfer all your property to a trust.

Often the job simply doesn't get done properly. People who conduct seminars to sell a product don't get paid to see that the titles of your property are changed or that the beneficiaries of your IRA account are changed. That is another distinction between financial planners who sell a product and financial consultants who don't.

In summary, financial consultants have a great deal of skill at gathering quantitative and qualitative information. They present to their clients objective financial plans, and they receive a reasonable compensation to see that those recommendations get implemented.

———•———

Your objective is to have enough money to last a lifetime.

"With all thy getting,
get understanding"

Sharon and John thought they had planned really well, but Sharon realizes now they hadn't. The ideal situation for a married couple is to identify a qualified financial consultant to conduct thorough, objective financial planning *before something happens*.

If the job has been done well, what happens in the event of the death of one spouse has been discussed so often and in such detail that the survivor is financially prepared. Then the greater issue at the time of death is the emotional one, the grief itself. If the financial issues have been laid out, the legal documents put in place, the strategies evaluated and understood by all parties, few questions arise. You simply stick to the plan. Developing a plan during your lifetime is an obvious way to avoid a tremendous amount of difficulty.

The financial circumstances appropriate for a man and wife are more than likely not appropriate for a widow alone. Sharon's joint ownership and other business matters are very typical. When John was living, the business agreements and the decision-making process were appropriate. But now they are inappropriate for — in fact, at odds with — Sharon's situation. If I had been advising John Trusty, I would have told him we needed to devise a mechanism that would allow Sharon to unwind from all these business arrangements in case he died before she did. We would have hired an attorney, committed the plan to a written agreement, established funding for life insurance, and communicated to all parties how the plan would work. Within six months after John's death, the plan could have been executed completely: Sharon would have had all her assets in a checking account. Then she could have gone forward from that point to construct her financial future.

A financial consultant must not assume that a couple's estate plan is an appropriate financial strategy for a widow. Unless a plan was carefully developed and currently revised, the consultant must assume that a widow's new circumstances require a new plan or strategy. And the widow must start acquiring the tools, the experience, the know-how, the understanding to set up a financial structure that will work for her.

Wisdom is the principle thing: therefore get wisdom: and with all thy getting get understanding.
— Proverbs 4:77

There is always confusion in the mind of a survivor. I can distinctly remember the first meeting with Gloria Plumlee after Carroll died. It hadn't been long at all since the three of us had worked to develop plans and strategies; still I had to ask her, "Now do you remember what we discussed about this trust?" She was simply unable to focus on those things. Even with the best planning, the emotions associated with the loss of a spouse overwhelm logic. But if you have planned well, you can always go back to your plan and read it. It's all there in writing.

Without question, a widow needs to have a trusted financial advisor. Even if the plan is to call a financial advisor after the first death, plan to use a *qualified* financial advisor. If no plan was made prior to death, it's best to call your advisor immediately. You don't want to make decisions without an overall strategy. Some decisions are irrevocable, and others should happen at a particular time and in a particular order. A good advisor will help the widow avoid inappropriate decisions immediately after the death. Remember, the only decision that must be made immediately is to determine who will help file the estate tax return.

Good planning takes time. The financial consultant must gather the quantitative and qualitative information in order to develop a plan. In the atmosphere of loss and grief, the job is much more difficult. For example, questions related to investment risk are answered differently before the spouse dies than they are answered soon after—if you can get answers at all. Moreover, these attitudes change dramatically until a widow finds she has both feet on the ground. It may take three weeks, three months, or three years to get to a point where the advisor can properly advise a client about investments. But there is no doubt that the process should begin immediately.

Perhaps without even realizing it, the widow has selected the decision partner to help deal with the problem of everyone telling her what she *should* do. When someone loses a spouse, family and friends bring lots of food, and after that they bring lots of advice. She can tell all her would-be advisors, "If you want to talk to me about what I should do with my business or my financial matters, you have to talk to me and my financial consultant together." Or, "I don't feel like talking about this today. You may call my advisor and express these opinions." This is a good answer for well-meaning yet unqualified friends and family members and also for those with inappropriate sales pitches. You can tell even the most well-meaning advisors: "Thank you, but I am working with my financial consultant on those decisions."

Of course, we're assuming the advisor to the widow has been interviewed and qualified. The advisor has the qualifications, the objectivity, the skill, the experience to get the job done. And the widow knows her consultant is not acting autonomously. That these are joint decisions. That the two of them are a team. That they are decision partners.

Should the widow feel that the financial consultant is not being objective or confidential or is making unilateral decisions, she should address her concerns immediately. The widow has to have absolute confidence and trust in the financial consultant. If she doesn't have it, she needs to find another financial consultant.

Confidentiality and discretion are very important. Several years ago I worked with a doctor's son, and he recommended me to his father. Not only was the father's quantitative information sensitive, but certain qualitative information was extremely sensitive.

For this retiring doctor, there were many decisions to be made. He had to be quite candid with me about his attitude toward his children. I was given information that could damage a family relationship that had been delicately forged over the years. He wanted none of his financial information to be known to anyone. After a couple of years the father and the son told me that they were amazed I could be so involved with working for each of them and never divulge any information to the other.

In addition to confidentiality, another basic tenet of a good consultant is objectivity. I describe it as being *beside* my client rather than on the other side of the table. I mentally draw a line. My client and I are on one side of that line. On the other side are financial products, financial services, financial institutions, legal services, accounting services — financial decisions of every sort. I help guide my client through this complex maze where a decision in one area invariably affects other areas. One of the key roles of a financial consultant is to intercept and communicate the onslaught of information coming through the press, radio, mail, and telephone. As I've suggested above, the sales rhetoric must be contended with. The financial consultant is an advocate, a defender of his client.

How I am compensated helps with this. Whether I am paid a percentage of assets or an hourly fee, the fiduciary responsibility to my client remains clear to me. I have an allegiance, a loyalty to my client, not to an institution. Of the seventy clients I serve, no two are alike. Their portfolios, their financial needs are not the same at all. It is a sign of how complex the times have become.

Good salespersons have real concern for clients and will serve them well. They keep their clients if they are doing good work. Still, the financial consultant is on the other side of that hypothetical line from them. Remember: salespersons are trained to get sales. The point is that salespersons and institutions are trained to be very good at arriving at *the* solution to client's problems — a solution that will require buying more of their product.

Independent financial consultants, on the other hand, are trained to use their time and expertise to help clients make decisions for themselves. Their role is to objectively assess their client's situation. It's not a matter of thinking that life insurance, stocks, bonds, mutual funds are inappropriate. In fact I recommend them; they are almost always part of what a client needs. But I like to look at the big picture, covering all the details with the client until she understands. We discuss the advantages and disadvantages of each idea or proposal logically and objectively.

The two processes are very different. The financial consultant helps the client make a decision in an informed environment without sales rhetoric. And there's nothing like competition. After a client and I have decided precisely what financial product is best, she can select the stockbroker or agent she wants to work with. But sometimes it's a good idea to call three or four companies and let them compete for the client's business.

When the client has enough information and enough time, she will understand. When she understands, she will be able to make a decision. Depending on the situation and the client, getting understanding may take only one session or only a phone call. It may take two or three sessions. But in time the decision comes. When it comes, the financial consultant calls up the salesperson: "The client is ready for your part now." The client has made the decision without emotion, without sales pitch, without pressure. We use the same process with tax services, with legal strategies, with bank loans, and with banking services—all these financial decisions.

It's important to ask how many clients a potential financial consultant is working with. The financial consultant has to have a lot of information to do this work well. He or she must read and learn, studying all the major financial areas: finance, law, tax, investments, and estate planning. My credentials require that I get twenty hours of continuing education credits each year; I usually get fifty or sixty. But it's a combination of experience and education that gives the consultant a grasp on everything. Hence, there is a limit to the number of clients he or she can serve well.

A financial consultant provides integration. He or she knows the client needs an accountant, an attorney, a banker, an insurance agent, a stockbroker, a real estate agent—all these professionals. The situation is like a puzzle; the financial consultant helps the client put the pieces together. A good financial consultant's forte is knowing when to bring in an attorney, when to bring in the insurance agent, the bank trust officer, the loan officer. It is something like being the conductor for a symphony orchestra.

This interaction is very positive for these other professionals as well. It's very efficient for them. For example, an insurance agent shows me various products; I review and discuss them with my client; the product is either a proper fit or not; I communicate to the agent that he does or does not get the sale. If he gets the sale, all he has to do is get the policy issued.

Working with stockbrokers is much the same. I call them and say, "We are going to invest ten thousand dollars today. We want you to show us superior-performing, large-company stocks that are paying a high dividend and are less volatile than the market as a whole." I am very specific about the types of investments that fit the portfolio. It is easy for the broker to talk with a financial consultant.

The attorneys, accountants, and bankers with whom I work save time also. They know my client is informed when she goes to them for advice. She can meet with them and discuss the matters with understanding.

A financial consultant provides integration...
like a symphony conductor.

You begin to rely
on someone again

When you are thrust into a totally different environment, it is always awkward until you gain experience and cultivate your own personal information. As you do this, things become more comfortable.

As a financial consultant, I know I'm accomplishing something when I'm communicating. And if I am good at this work, I can see when the client and I really are communicating. That usually takes a long time with a widow, but then there will be a moment when a light goes on—a little bit more information, a little bit more experience, and the work becomes productive.

Over time, the clients become acclimated, become less awkward. The client may not know all the technical terms, she may not understand all the issues, but our level of communication is at a point where awkwardness recedes and is replaced by understanding and, eventually, a tremendous sense of financial security.

Certainly there has to be a change in the way that you approach financial decisions. In Sharon's case, she has a business partner. Until John died, her relationship with Bill had been social; she didn't interact with him on business. Now, over a period of time, she has discovered that she has to deal with him on a different basis. Now it is business: she has to discuss tax issues, contractual issues, and financial issues.

She has crossed an important threshold: as she is equipped with knowledge, she can sit down and have a business conversation with him. This is not to say he won't be her friend anymore, but now she sits down with him in the capacity of business partner, and they have business to discuss. It's a matter, first, of recognizing she is going to work with him on that basis, and, second, of gaining the information she needs to make those business decisions. Those are important changes—and I'm sure she has a profound sense she is giving something up. Her relationship with him will never be the same. It's a passage.

So for Sharon, the awkwardness and the unfamiliarity of the business world are slowly giving way to experience; she is becoming familiar with money and risk and taxes and can communicate about those things.

When you reach that point with an advisor—a decision partner—it becomes fulfilling because you begin to rely on someone again. You have confidence that your decision partner is there to "catch you," that things are not going to fall through the cracks. You don't have nearly as much fear. You have control, you have awareness, you have information, but you don't have fear.

One of my clients still doesn't understand the more technical aspects of designing an investment portfolio, but when we talk now, we're communicating. She understands. She doesn't need to know all the nuances of Modern Portfolio Theory to understand her finances. She has come to know how and why I make recommendations to her. She knows there is probably not a question concerning her financial situation for which I don't have the answer or at least have access to the answer. She knows that a dependable decision partner is there.

Being able to depend on somebody else makes you feel a lot more comfortable. It makes the fear evaporate. I don't think you ever get to that point unless you have a lot of confidence in your decision partner. If the relationship is properly structured, you are never *dependent* upon that person, but that person is *dependable*.

I need clients to be dependable too. The relationship has to be very free and open—a two-way street. I have the same expectations of clients as they have of me.

A friend of mine who's a surgical nurse says she is amazed to see patients for their second, third, even fourth heart bypass surgery. Those patients have kept the old habits of eating cheeseburgers and fries, smoking—maybe throwing down a few beers. You can't keep doing the same old things you were doing and get healthy.

I depend on the client's making changes to move forward. Both client and advisor need to be dependable.

The event of widowhood radically changes a woman's life. It is something she never gets over completely. Some learn from it, learn to let go of it, but it's never really gone.

I believe Sharon will find some harmony with it. She'll find— after a matter of months or years—that she gets her answers and resolves many issues. And she'll look back on this period of time, this three or four years after her husband passed away, and she will see it as a dark, difficult time. But she will get past that and come away with a whole new set of experiences—experiences in which she chooses people to work with her and makes financial decisions. She will be treated fairly.

Whatever she wants to accomplish in her life, she will know what her limitations are financially; she'll know what she can do and what she can't. She'll know how to make financial decisions without agonizing over them. She will know how to use decision partners to make fully informed decisions. She'll get to the point where she has a healthy financial perspective—a big part of her overall well-being.

Beginning Again

———◆———

Sharon:
*I've decided not to call it a new life;
I'm trying to call it a different life.*

I had been floating
from distraction to distraction

I had been floating from distraction to distraction. I felt I had been cut loose from my moorings. When I started working with Barry, I began a period of discovery.

Up to this point, I had a fear, a total lack of knowledge. I had confidence in my ability to learn, but somebody else had been tying my shoes for me. Barry asked me what I wanted to work on first. There were many choices: how do I turn some of my assets into income? How does the insurance trust work? What are my state and federal tax obligations? How does my IRA work? What do I need to do about retirement income? House insurance, auto insurance, personal property taxes, insurance on my real estate holdings?

The first thing I wanted to do was to get my *own* will and trust documents drawn up. I did not want anyone, especially my children, to have to deal with what I was dealing with. While the attorney was working on those documents, Barry asked me to gather all my deeds and titles and we made plans to discuss each one. This was something tangible I could work with — and that alone made things more manageable. As Barry explained each document I gave him, I felt a new freedom.

When you don't understand something, you can't remember it; it's like trying to take Algebra II without having had Algebra I. You muddle through and you muddle through, but until you learn Algebra I, you won't be able to understand Algebra II. It was only after I began to understand, that the confusion started to disappear.

It was pointed out to me that I had to learn to make decisions with my head and not my heart. One of those decisions was who to do business with. Though I was ready to move forward, some of my well-meaning advisors could not acknowledge the changes

John's death had brought about in my circumstances. They could not see me without my husband.

I had to break away from some thirty-year friendships and business associations. It was hard. I discovered, though, that working with people who never knew John, who know me now and my circumstances as they are *now,* is much easier. My new advisors believe I *should* handle my own business matters. And with my new advisors, there's no past, no prejudice; they are working with me in the present.

I began enjoying the confidence I gained working with Barry. I quickly realized he was not selling a product. Almost everyone else had been trying to sell me a product; each one had tried to convince me that his or her product was exactly what I needed. Insurance people wanted to sell annuities; stockbrokers wanted to sell me stock; brokerage firms wanted to sell me mutual funds.

They approached my needs from a product point of view: their product was exactly what I needed. An independent financial advisor approaches it from a needs perspective. Barry sat down with me and helped me determine what my individual needs were, then we went searching for the products and services that would meet my needs.

Every widow's or widower's needs are different, depending on age, income, retirement status, etc. But there is a common need, and that is the need to take care of these matters. Barry has said, "The best way to be a widow is to take care of arrangements ahead of time, with your husband's help. But the reality is that most people don't preplan well. The next best solution is to find a good decision partner to help you navigate this territory called widowhood."

Doing either of these will give the widow more strength and resources to devote to the actual work of grief. Part of that work is coming into the present. You cannot move out of the past when people shield you from the present. And every widow needs to face the present.

I was about to experience
the healing of my thought life

When my kids had gone through different problems as teenagers, I had taken them to counseling. It was very helpful, but for some reason I didn't think of counseling for myself. I thought I was handling my grief well enough on my own.

It was only after things started happening — like having blurred vision and not wanting to be around my kids — that I had to admit I wasn't doing as well as I thought I was. I didn't realize it then, but I think I wanted someone to carry the burden of stress and grief for me. Since I couldn't have that, I thought having a counselor tell me how to do it myself might be the next best thing.

I knew I wanted a counselor who shared my basic beliefs, who would respect my belief in God. I didn't want anyone telling me my religious beliefs were a part of the problem. I was having a hard enough time with God as it was. And I didn't want someone to tell me that I needed to get out and find somebody to replace John.

I found a wonderful Christian counselor in Russellville named Jon Lundquist. After the first visit with Jon, I knew I could be comfortable. I knew I could share my pain with him. I had a list of things I wanted to work on with him. I told him, "I am so stressed, and I don't even have time to read a stress management book. I need your crash course."

His first assignment, though, was to get me through that second Christmas. I thought I was absolutely going to die. Even the Christmas songs I heard playing everywhere were unbearable. I couldn't understand it because we had made it through the first Christmas; I realize now that during that time we had had the blessing of shock. Shock can give a temporary illusion of peace. My kids were all there the first Christmas; they came that Christmas Eve and spent the night. We had a "slumber party." But by that second Christmas, reality was sinking in.

All along I had been talking about how I *felt:* I felt stressed; I felt selfish; I felt that God didn't love me. So Jon addressed my feelings first of all. On that first visit he suggested to me that I had delayed the process of grieving. He said one of the biggest needs in grief is to feel what you feel. The first months I had the construction workers there, and when I felt something, I had to hide it. When I felt something in front of my kids, I had to hide it. So Jon told me it was time for me to go home and feel what I felt. He said, "Express and acknowledge your feelings. If you feel the urge to cry, you cry. Those feelings are inside of you, and they are going to stay there until they come out, and they will come out at some point in your life, in some form or fashion." He continued, "The next time you hear a Christmas carol, sit down and feel what you feel." So I did. I cried. I did that two or three times, and after that it was OK. Before Christmas came, I was better. Christmas was still very hard, but at least I had begun to acknowledge my feelings.

What I was about to experience was the healing of my thought life. The book of Proverbs teaches, "As a man thinketh in his heart, so is he." Negative feelings often begin with negative thoughts. If I could identify the negative thoughts, then I could modify the negative feelings. Jon taught me to express and acknowledge those feelings, but not to let my feelings necessarily motivate my behavior.

Jon told me to trust my own system to work for me, to follow it and to stop trying to make it follow me. I had made that mistake when I said, "All right, I'm going to give myself one year to grieve. It's going to be like a job. Any time I need to grieve, that will come first." I was trying to make grief follow me.

With Jon, I developed a list of some of my "counterfeit" feelings. For example, guilt: there are two kinds of guilt—real guilt and false guilt. Jon taught me to identify which kind of guilt I was feeling. That really helped me in my relationships—because at that time so many people wanted some of my time. When I applied the idea of counterfeit feelings, I could see that real guilt is when somebody *needs* me and I'm not there and that false guilt is if somebody just *wants* me there. He taught me to ask myself, "Do they *need* me or do they *want* me?"

He also pointed out that there are facts, and then there are feelings. One time I said, "I just don't feel like God loves me!" He said, "Is that a fact or a feeling?" He told me there are a lot of fact-versus-feelings issues involved in happiness. He said that I had to make up my mind to be happy no matter what, that I could choose to stop placing conditions on my happiness.

I didn't know I was doing that. But I began to realize how I had been thinking: I could be happy *if only* Jessica and Robert weren't divorcing; I could be happy *if only* Jonna and Scot weren't moving away.

Over time I would see Jon around town, at Rotary meetings, and to tell the truth, it made me uncomfortable that I was still struggling and grieving. So I found a counselor in Little Rock, Jean Speegle. Jean suggested that I read *The Feeling Good Handbook* by Dr. David Burns. In it, Burns identifies ten negative thought patterns. He suggests that people tend to hone in on two or three favorites. I was faithfully practicing about eight of them! For instance, predicting the future: there was a message on my answering machine one day from Willa, the bookkeeper at Russellville Steel: "Mrs. Trusty, I need you to call me." Predicting what she wanted, I thought, *Oh, she is going to want me to come out there and sign a check, and I don't have time to do that today.* But when I called her, she said, "I've got a package out here for you." I said, "OK, I'll drop by in a few days and pick it up."

Recognizing these negative thought patterns helped me take back control and manage my stress. Jon had pointed out to me some key phrases: *I have to. I should have. What if.* Other thoughts can relieve stress: *I've done the best I can, and as a rule I do pretty well.*

I began to deprogram and reprogram based on these concepts my counselors taught me. When I would go to see Jon or Jean, I would take a notebook; I looked on what they told me as homework. I really practiced what they suggested. When I would catch myself feeling frantic or negative, I would stop and ask myself what was going on with my thinking; each time I was able to identify some thought or way of thinking that had triggered the negative response.

Another important factor in dealing with stress is taking care of your body. For instance, you must honor your sleep needs. I was not doing that. And I had let exercise fall by the wayside. I felt guilty taking the time to exercise because I felt I had so many *important* things I needed to be doing. Jon told me that exercise, like sleep, is a survival need. It produces endorphins in the brain that have a calming effect. In addition, I learned that some of the chemicals produced by stress can only be broken down by exercise. (Some people say some of these come out in tears, that crying is healing.) I justified taking time to exercise by telling myself I was taking care of my body so my children wouldn't have to take care of me. I always felt that I had to justify everything, but that's another thing I learned—I don't have to.

Jon told me not to tell myself that there is not enough time. Later Jean and I worked on my schedule. I found if I made an appointment with myself, I could get around to exercising and doing a lot of things I thought I didn't have time for. I put them on the calendar. She suggested I make a list and commit a certain amount of time to complete a certain task. That way I would focus on the time instead of the fact that I didn't get it completed. Before I used this technique all I could see was what I wasn't getting done.

I had always been proud of my ability to pace myself. But I found I wasn't doing a very good job of that either. There was too much to do! Have you ever worked in the yard until you were too tired to put the tools up? You need to stop thirty minutes before you get completely exhausted to do all of that. But I would just work until I couldn't go any further—and still the doors needed to be locked and the cat needed to be fed and the lights had to be turned out. So I had to pace myself and learn to honor my body's signals. I now see that if I feel well physically, I can deal with almost anything; but if I'm tired, it's so much harder. So taking care of myself has to be a priority.

Once I went to see Jean and told her, "I have to get a handle on worry. I worry all the time, about everything." She told me to make an appointment with myself to worry. She said, "How much time do you need to worry? An hour a day?" I said, "I don't have time to worry an hour a day."

She said, "OK, how about an hour a week?"

I said, "OK," and assumed we were finished.

But she asked, "What day?"

I thought a moment and answered, "Friday is a good day because it is before the weekend and I'm usually in a better mood."

So she said, "For one hour on Fridays you are going to worry."

"OK."

"What is a good time for you?"

I said, "Nine in the morning ."

So Jean said, "OK. You are going to worry every week from nine to ten on Friday mornings. Now, I want you to categorize your worries, and I want you to do it this way. When a worry creeps into your mind, place it in one of these categories: things you absolutely can't do anything about; things in which you might be able to effect some minimal change; things you definitely can take care of. The ones you can't do anything about, toss them immediately. Never let them back in. Put the other two aside for Friday."

Going along with her, I said, "OK, then what do I do?"

"On Friday you use your nine-to-ten hour to make a plan about what you are going to do about those things."

I said, "But some things just won't wait. They'll be gone by Friday."

Jean just looked at me and grinned. "Oh," I said. "OK."

I told her I didn't want to become a person who is irresponsible, who doesn't face reality, who pushes everything aside. She said, "I think you are being very responsible; you have just made an appointment to take care of your worries." So I did that, and it worked. There have even been some weeks when I have forgotten to worry on Friday from nine to ten.

———◆———

For as a man thinketh in his heart, so is he.
—Proverbs 23:77

It's like a slow rain

Both counselors told me they didn't think I had said good-bye. So Jon and I came up with a plan. I was to write John a letter and go through our whole relationship, from the first time I threw a spit wad at him in my ninth grade science class until he died. When I went home to write it, though, I couldn't because I said to myself, "I don't have anybody to replace him." I was of the mind that you don't give something up until you have something better to replace it with. So I just cried and left it at that.

I went back and asked Jon, "How can I give him up or say goodbye to him before I have somebody to replace him with?" I wasn't even dating.

He said, "No, Sharon, you mustn't do that. You need to resolve your feelings in that relationship and learn to be happy with yourself first. Because if you don't, there will always be three people in any new relationship." I had never thought about that. He was right.

Originally I went to see Jean about Jessica and Robert's divorce—another personal loss to me—but then I started telling her some things about myself. I told her that I didn't understand why I was still having such a big problem with my husband's death. After a couple of visits, she said to me "Sharon, I don't think you know who you are." I thought, "This is great. I'm over fifty and I'm trying to find out who I am."

But I learned she was right. I knew who I was when my husband was alive. But this was a different life. I didn't know myself as a businesswoman; I didn't know myself as a single woman (I hadn't had a date in over thirty years); I didn't know myself as a single parent. Or as a plumber, gardener, investor—or in many other roles in which I now found myself. She told me this would be a period of self-discovery.

My counselors had told me I couldn't put conditions on happiness. If I based my happiness on John's being here, that was putting a condition on it. If my happiness depended on Jessica and Robert's solving their marital difficulties, that was putting a condition on it.

I simply have to accept reality as it is, not as I would like it to be. I simply have to accept whatever is.

I had said, "I'll grieve for one year and that will be enough." And that one day I would tell myself, "OK, that's enough; I'll quit grieving today. It's time to be over it and move forward, and that's what I'm going to do." But Jon told me, "You can't do that. You don't make grief follow you; you have to follow it. It's like a slow rain."

I learned in the grief therapy class the funeral home offered that grief is a series of goodbyes. First there's the loss; then shock. Then you come out of it a little, and then something else happens. If you are a woman, it might be something trivial like your car doesn't start. Then you feel the loss all over and go back down. Then you realize, "I can call a friend," or "I can call a wrecker and get it towed in." Then you do better for a while, until the next goodbye. A man might realize he doesn't know how to cook. He'll experience the loss and spiral down, and he'll have to say goodbye. Then he'll realize he can go to a local restaurant. And each time the lows are not quite as low as they were the last time, and finally you just give yourself permission to stop grieving. Like a slow rain soaking in.

Your solution to grief is just another way of giving the same answer that God gave me in the first empty days—accept this. Only in acceptance lies peace—not in forgetting nor in resignation nor in busy-ness.

—Elisabeth Elliott, in a letter
to Catherine Marshall,
quoted in *Beyond Ourselves*

People kept telling me I had to build a new life, but to me that meant I had to give up the old. I didn't want new. I wanted my old life back.

I had had a life I loved. I kept trying to go back to it, but when I did, it wasn't there. This made my life unfamiliar. I was rebellious: I was going to stay right where I was because I liked it and I wanted to be there. I couldn't go back because there wasn't anything to go back to, but I was also afraid of the future. I was stuck.

Then one night I was driving home from Little Rock—I had been there to check on Jessica, who had the flu. I wanted to fix her some soup, so I had gone to the grocery store. I was in this strange grocery store. Jessica had rented a house in Maumelle, and I was walking into this strange house, not her house in Russellville. And her boyfriend, Chuck, was there, and he was not Robert. My whole life felt like a dream world. Driving home, I just said a little prayer. I realized then that the present had to become the *familiar* and where I had been—the past—had to become the *unfamiliar*. Wherever I was had to be familiar. I think that is acceptance.

As I began to follow my grief instead of trying to make it follow me, I realized that I didn't have to leave my friends, I didn't have to leave my memories, but I needed to add. I was really fortunate in having some friends who moved along with me. The friends who didn't were the ones who couldn't accept the changes brought about by my circumstances. They wanted us to go on interacting as we always had. It was possible for them to continue as always, but not for me. They probably still don't realize they were asking for me and my old life back. I would have loved to be able to give it to them. The friends who really helped me moved forward with me. They took the attitude, "OK, half of you is gone, we'll just take the half that's left, make the necessary adjustments, and move on with you."

When things would get so unbearable I couldn't stand it, I would just crawl up in the middle of my bed and wait to die. I knew I wouldn't die; I just refused to do anything—couldn't do anything—to go on during those times. I didn't want to go on, but I wanted to want to.

New Year's Eve 1997, three-and-a-half years after John died, was one of those times. I was watching a movie about Ted Bundy, the serial killer. In the movie, the parents of one of his victims had been called to the police station to identify a body the police thought might be their daughter's. When they got there, the father said to the mother, "You wait here; I'll go do this." The camera stayed on her face, but you could hear him off camera screaming, "Oh, dear God, no!" And the mother just stood still with tears streaming down her face.

I said to them, to the television, "You can survive this. You don't know it now, but you will survive this." Then I realized I was talking to myself.

That was the first time I really knew I could survive because I had made the choice to do so. If I were asked to define *acceptance,* I would say it is finally knowing that you cannot change some of your circumstances. I could not change death. And that night I stopped struggling to do so. When you stop struggling to do something you cannot do, there is great relief. I think that's what acceptance is.

I have accepted John's death. I haven't gotten this "new life thing" down yet. But I've decided not to call it a new life. I'm trying to call it a different life.

But this one thing I do,
forgetting those things which are behind,
and reaching forth unto those things which are before.
—Philippians 3:13

It's hard to date
when you're fifty

The best treatment for widowhood, according to conventional wisdom, is: *Here's a covered dish. Now you need to start dating.* To some people, the fact that I was not dating, engaged, or remarried meant I was not "getting on with my life." In other words, I wasn't working hard enough to move forward. When I first started to consider dating, it was because of pressure from family and friends who probably thought that dating would result in remarriage, the end of grief, the end of confusion. There was no way for me to know if they were right or wrong.

I hated the term *widow,* until one night at church when some of my friends were encouraging me to sign up for the annual Christmas party. "Come on, Sharon. It'll be so much fun." "You can sit with us." "Bring a friend." Finally I said I would sign up, and I asked where the sign-up sheet was. When I found the sign-up sheet, I saw the headings COUPLES and SINGLES. That was when I decided I didn't like the term *single* either. I went back to being a widow.

For that matter, I was uncomfortable with the word *dating.* Fifty-year-old women don't date. Fifty-year-old women don't have boyfriends. I don't know what fifty-year-old women do have. But whatever it is, I have decided that it is an important part of the process of healing and moving forward. I'll tell you why.

Although I've had lots of friends, I have only really dated one person. As with all other issues regarding grief, people handle dating in their own ways. Different people have different timelines, and different reasons for dating. For example, a person divorced or widowed who no longer loves their spouse might start to date sooner. A person who has children has to take the feelings of her children into consideration. I wanted my kids to be comfortable seeing me with someone else. I didn't think it would matter whether I waited six months or ten years, when they saw me with another man it was going to require some major adjustments on their parts.

They didn't know this. About six months after John died, my daughters gave me permission to date. They came to me and said, "Mom, we know Dad's gone. We don't want you to stay home all the time by yourself." They knew it was hard for me, and they were being kind. They knew I was sad and thought it would help. I tried not to show how sad I was, but most people would say, "I can see it in your eyes." So my daughters gave me permission to date. I thanked them, and said "I'll probably have to remind you of this someday." That day came.

There were several men who, because of their reputations, I expected would be calling. One day, when Katherine was at my house, one of them called and asked me to go to dinner with him. I told him I wasn't dating. But I went out to the kitchen and said excitedly, "That was Paul! He asked me to go to dinner with him Friday!"

Katherine's mouth dropped open. She turned white and said, "Mom! He was Dad's friend! He used to eat breakfast with Dad; he went fishing with Dad! How can he ask you out?"

I just let her rant. Then I grinned and said, "What happened to 'Mom, it's OK with us if you go out with men'? Kathy, even if I wait ten years, you are going to feel this way."

Lately they have been more insistent. My son-in-law Bruce introduced me to a pilot who has a house in San Francisco and one in Dallas. Later I called and left a message on Bruce and Katherine's answering machine: "Now when Pete and I get married, I need to know if we're going to live in San Francisco or in Dallas?" My girls wanted me to promise I wouldn't move away from Russellville! The other day I told them that if I did fall in love with someone, and he lived, say, in Utah, that I would move to Utah in a heartbeat. My children don't try to run my life, and if they did, I wouldn't let them. But I do think I have to take their feelings into consideration. And I have.

I think it's important to be honest with yourself about some things. Why are you dating? Do you want a friend? Do you want a romance? Are you lonely? Are you dating someone because he has pressured you to go out with him?

It's hard to date when you're fifty! One problem I had early on was that I flattered myself. When somebody asked me to go to lunch or for a cup of coffee, I would refuse, thinking his motive was romantic, and I did not want a romance yet. I've learned since that some people are just being friendly or kind; they may just want to be friends. Today if someone asks me out, I assume that what he wants is friendship only. I treat him as I treat my girlfriends, and for the most part, it's what they want.

A few have wanted to become romantically involved, and when it didn't happen, it seemed to hurt their feelings and I lost their friendship. Those situations bothered me so much I talked to Jean about them. Her advice was, "Be honest with them, and remember you should not and cannot accept responsibility for someone else's feelings."

Dating can be one of the most traumatic stages of moving forward — especially when you're older and out of practice. Often I felt like I did when I was in high school and the "right" guy didn't ask me to the ballgame. Or when someone had a crush on me and called me five times a day, or didn't want me to go with anyone else, or didn't understand that I was busy. Only this time, I was fifty years old, and had a lot of other matters that needed my attention. And most important, John Trusty was the only one I wanted to be with.

I like male companionship; I have always had male friends. But I began to miss having someone to make me want to put on makeup, to get a haircut — a flirtatious, romantic interest. At the same time, I had learned to make myself numb. I didn't want to feel again because it was too risky. But I didn't want to become one of those people who shut down and never feel the good things, either. I was a mass of contradictions: *I want to feel, but not to hurt; I don't want to be lonely, but there's nobody I want to be with.*

In this time of extreme vulnerability, it is easy to make mistakes. It is almost like "love deprivation syndrome." It's not sexual. You miss *human contact* — someone to hold, and to hold you.

Someone to hug you. Someone special. I recall telling my children, "You know, if I could find someone who would just live in the bedroom on the other end of the house, I'd marry him." I wouldn't have, of course, but for the first time in my life, I understood why and how some women make the mistakes they make. Loneliness, I think, is worse than the loss. With the loss, the pain dulls, but loneliness never dulls: it is fresh and sharp every time it hits you. I knew that I must be careful about what I did in the name of loneliness.

I was beginning to see how a person might love again

I am thankful God didn't send me anyone during those first months—because I think if someone had shown some interest in me, had been affectionate with me, I probably would have thought I loved him. For eighteen months I had no desire to even talk to a man. I was lonely, but dating or being involved with someone didn't seem like a solution. I felt that in order to love anyone again, I had to be willing to lose again. And I wasn't. I had decided I was willing to give up feeling the good stuff just to make certain that I could avoid ever again feeling pain like I had felt. If it hadn't been for Bob Taylor, that's exactly where I would have stayed.

John and I had known Bob for years. John once told me, "That Bob Taylor is a good man." Bob had been divorced about eleven years. He owned several businesses in Russellville, one of which was a landscape business. It was about this time that I discovered the therapeutic benefits of gardening and began spending a lot of time in my yard. Sometimes when I was in the yard, he would pass by and stop to ask how I was doing. I found that he was very sensitive and able to identify with some of the stages of loss I was going through because they were similar to some things he'd been through with his divorce. We would sit and talk, sometimes for hours; sometimes I would even cry. It wasn't long before I felt I could pour my heart out to Bob.

One evening I realized how much I enjoyed talking with him, and I asked him if he wanted to stay for dinner. All I had to offer was bacon and eggs, but he had a County Fair Board meeting that night. So we made plans to have dinner a couple of nights later. The next day after our dinner date he called to tell me how much he enjoyed it. I told him I had enjoyed it too, and he asked me to go to dinner with him the next Saturday. I was surprised—I really wanted to! I don't know if I was surprised he asked me or surprised I wanted to go. Either way, it was nice.

My friends Bill and Vicky, Kerri and Gary, and I always spent Saturday evenings together, and I began wondering what I would tell them. I was very nervous about telling them, and I didn't understand why. But they were excited and happy about it. They teased me about coming over to the house to give Bob a hard time. I was afraid they really would. I told them I'd better not see any of them.

Then Saturday a strange thing happened. I woke up and started thinking about my first "date." I started crying and couldn't stop. I called Vicky, and Kerri was at her house. I told them I couldn't go out on this date, that it felt like I was committing adultery. They said, "Sharon, you are going to have to do this someday—why not now? Bob is so nice." There was a Razorback football game on; so I asked them if they wanted to come over to watch the game. Then I called Bob and told him I had some friends who wanted to watch the game on my big screen television. I asked him if it would be OK if we did that instead of going out. He said, "Sure."

After the game, when everyone else had left, Bob asked me, "Is this the first time you have been with someone in front of your friends?" He said I was so nervous that he knew.

Even after that, it was difficult for me to go out with Bob in public for a long time. It was like I was announcing to the world, "Hey, I'm over John now. I'm through with John, and I'm moving on." But without my realizing it, the pain began to recede and some of the loneliness began to go away.

If it hadn't been for Bob Taylor, I may have just shut down. It was good to have somebody call and check on me. It was good to have somebody call when I went to Little Rock to see if I had made it home all right, or ask me to call him to say I had arrived safely. I felt protected and cared for. I began to notice I *could* feel those kinds of warm feelings again. Bob is very unassuming; he has a quiet strength about him. Although I will never compare anyone to John, I know I look for certain qualities in a man: honesty, integrity, decency. Bob has those qualities. And he is a good father. His sons, Chris and Robert, are his whole life.

I was beginning to see how a person might love again. I had read that the first relationship after a loss can be devastating. I was lucky to have Bob. He understood what I was dealing with better than I understood it myself. That was very important, especially in a first relationship. He didn't pressure me; he didn't smother or hover. He wasn't looking for a commitment, just friendship. Bob has played a major part in my healing process. Sometimes the healing has been subtle. I don't remember when I stopped thinking about John's death the first thing when I woke up each morning. And I don't remember when I realized that sometimes I was thinking of someone else when I woke up.

I really haven't dated very much because it's too much trouble. It has seemed to take too much out of me. I have needed all my energies and resources to deal with more important issues. Dating seemed to create havoc with my already disorganized life. And I had never been intimidated going out alone. Then one night at a charity fundraiser I had a bad experience: I discovered people treat you differently when you are unescorted. An unescorted woman, in the eyes of some, is wearing a sign that reads, "Here I am!"

I have observed that society treats a widow with more respect than a divorcée. In fact, there are different attitudes for every class of single person: never married, under thirty never married, over thirty, with children, without children, widowed, divorced, and so on. In this respect, I felt lucky to be a widow.

I was discussing all this with a friend, Jebb Young, one evening. Jebb is much younger than I am, but I've called on him many times to advise me. He has always understood my predicament. "Sharon," he said, "I watched my mom go through this. I think dating is OK; it's great for you. But do not get married. Even if you should meet someone you think you might want to marry, do not get married!" "Why?" I asked him.

"Because you are not yet the woman you are going to be. You're getting there, but you're not quite there yet. When this period of growth is finished, you are going to be a different person. And you

will really like who you are. You will be stronger, more knowledgeable, more capable, and whoever marries you will need to
know that woman. Or he will wake up one day and find himself
married to someone he hardly knows."

"Are you sure you want to heal? Do you really want to move forward?"

One day I said to Jean, "Your job assignment today is to help me learn to accept change." She asked me, "Are you sure you want to heal? Do you really want to move forward?"

I thought she was kidding. Of course I wanted to heal! I didn't want to hurt like this forever. But I knew she must have a good reason for asking. I thought about it and realized that in healing, I would be moving farther away from John, and I would have to decide to do just that if I ever wanted to move forward. I asked myself, *Do you really want to heal as badly as you think you do? Do you really want to move away from John?*

I think this is where most people get stuck in their grief. Grief requires that we both hang on and let go. To let go of what you're holding onto is scary. And so is moving forward because you can't move forward without leaving something behind. I didn't want to leave John, but I wanted to heal. There is no good in continuing to be in love with a dead man. Moving forward didn't mean I loved him less, or that I had forgotten him. It was just the healthy thing to do. I began moving forward when I chose to stop clinging to the past.

In darker days, I had thought, *I'll wait until I'm ready.* But when you're talking about the grief process, there are some things you may never be ready for. But after they are behind you, you discover it was good to go ahead, it was the right thing to do.

Some things, though, are easier if done step-by-baby-step. For example, I couldn't give away John's clothes. I was waiting to be "ready." First, I took them out of our bedroom closet and put them in another closet. Then, a while later, I boxed them up. They sat there until this past winter. One weekend Jonna came home for a visit. Late that night she came to me, and she was crying. "Mom," she said, "I want you to sleep on this tonight, and tomorrow unless you tell me not to, I'm going to take Dad's clothes away."

I wasn't ready, but I knew I should have been. The next morning I said,"Go ahead and take them." We both cried as we carried them to her car. Later she asked, "How do you feel, Mom?" I said, "I feel like I will never be happy again for the rest of my life." But a day or two later it was OK.

I don't know how you differentiate between things you should go ahead and do and things you should definitely not do—like getting married the first year or selling your house right away. Some seemingly small things were really big steps for me because each one brought a goodbye—changing the name on the charge accounts, credit cards, utilities, phone book, mailbox, checking account. I moved the furniture in the den because every time I walked into that room, I looked at John's chair expecting to see him sitting there. His truck was still parked in the driveway. I would walk down the hallway and look out the window and say, "Oh! John's home." Finally I called someone to come get the truck. Those are some changes I gradually made, and they helped me move from the past to the present.

I remember when I made up my mind to take off my wedding rings. I had shopped for years at Dillard's in Little Rock, and I was often helped by a saleslady who had been widowed twenty years. We would talk, and she'd ask, "How you doin', honey?" I'd say, "Well, it's just so hard." She'd cry, and I'd cry. One day as I drove home after one such visit, I started thinking, *Her husband has been dead for over twenty years. Am I going to be doing this twenty years from now?* I took my wedding rings off and I said, "John, I'm always going to love you, but I am not going to be *in love* with a dead man any longer."

One giant step I've taken was to lease an apartment in Little Rock. When John died, many things were so comforting to me, including my home. But at some point, the house—like many other things which were comforting in the beginning—ceased to be comforting and became painful. I don't even know when this occurred, but I realized one day that in my house, I was constantly reminded of what I had lost. I was trying to appreciate what I had; I was trying to count my blessings. So I decided to lease an apartment in Little Rock to baby-step my way into selling my house. It was very scary. I had some of the same feelings and worries I had when John died. But, again, it was the best thing to do.

At first I could look at photographs; then I couldn't. Remember the old jacket John loved, the one I put in the washer and dryer? I would get that out of the closet and wear it. It had his smell; it felt so good. That was good and comforting for a while, but all of a sudden when I did that I would cry. As I found things were making me sad instead of comforting me, I would stop doing them.

At first, I thought I could never be happy again; I just hoped the pain would go away. Now I am beginning to raise my expectations. I think that someday I might even find happiness without him, maybe even love again. I compare it to having your first child. You think you can never love another child that much, but when the second is born, you see that your love doubles, it grows. It is not halved. You just have more love to give.

I think it's the same way with life: I have more life to give. And who knows what life has to give me?

———•———

You cannot step twice into the same river,
for the water into which you first stepped has flowed on.
— Heraclitus

There is no way out of the canyon except down the river.
— Unknown

"Did you think you'd live to be ninety and never have a flat tire?"

I used to have an attitude about change: that everything good was permanent. That the things I wanted to last would last. Anything else was an interruption. Some of the best advice I've received has been from a friend of mine, Cindy Martin, who cuts my hair. She and I have become close confidantes, and one morning she said to me, "I thought of you this morning. When I was driving to work, the guy on the radio was talking about things not going smoothly in our lives — and about accepting them. He said, 'If you have a flat tire today, that's life. Did you think you would live to be ninety and never have a flat tire?'"

You've heard people say, "It's not what happens to you that's important; it's what you do about it." I have a choice about what I want to do with grief. Do I continue, or do I let it go? The process can only end when I'm willing to let it go.

The lessons that we learn from loss should make us better people, because through loss we can grow. The first thing I needed to know was that I was going to live. Next I had to believe it was OK to live. And finally, I need to believe I will be happy again. I have a lot of new opportunities.

You know the old story of the bundle of sticks: if you are given a bundle of sticks and you try to break all of them at the same time, you can't. But if you take one stick out at a time, you can break them all. It's the same way with solving problems, making decisions, and getting things done; it's the same with starting over. If you try to break all of the sticks at once, you end up not doing anything. Breaking things into smaller pieces makes impossible jobs possible. Breaking things down also helps you know your options.

Another thing I have decided is you don't have to know things to be smart. You just need to recognize what you don't know and then find someone to help you learn. Without realizing it, I think I used "not knowing" as a crutch, an excuse to put off making decisions and taking action, but I don't do that anymore. I am relieved by that discovery, and I have given myself permission to make decisions and take action.

Beginning again is a weeding-out process. I've added so many things to my life that I have had to weed out some things. At some point, maybe I can add some of them back in.

Jon Lundquist told me to start small when looking for joy. He and I had talked for a long time about how to find it. I told him I loved gardening, so I've started taking "vacation days": I put the answering machine on, buy six flats of flowers, and don't do anything else all day long.

I have changed my attitude about the learning I must do. I recall saying, "I don't have time to learn this; I just need to know it. I don't have time to learn how to be strong; I just need to be strong." But growth is developmental, and it is incremental. It can't be done suddenly; you lay a piece of groundwork, and you build on it incrementally.

I have started applying this knowledge to my life. I take joy where I find it, and I try each day to remember: *Accept what was, what is, and remember there is always hope unless I stop hoping.* I know my faith will play a significant role in my new beginning. I have accepted the past and now I am trying to accept the future. I now know that life won't always happen the way I think it should, but God is in control. I'm depending on Him to help me find new meaning.

When John died, he left me a job, a job for which I was not qualified. But as I understand my situation more and more, I find I'm beginning to enjoy my new role. I never would have chosen it, but I do find I'm liking it more. At some point I may actually love it.

I made my first big trip: I went to New York. Some things were a little poignant. When I got to Atlanta, I missed my connection. So I decided to take a plane to Washington and catch the shuttle on up to New York. I got on the plane and realized I was going to Washington, D.C. and no one in the whole wide world knew where I was. I found myself wanting to call home and tell some-one where I was. But I didn't.

I was meeting Jonna in New York, and she and I went to din-ner, attended plays, saw the sights. By the end of the week, we were giving directions to other tourists! We must have appeared to be confident: "Go down two blocks and turn right." The best thing I got out of the trip wasn't what we did; it was the realiza-tion that I was capable.

The apartment in Little Rock has helped me tremendously. It's a haven, a getaway. It has helped me realize that "different" is OK. I like changes that reflect the future instead of the past. This change will help me know where I want to build my new house. I feel capable of doing it now; after all, I completed the construc-tion project alone. I've started looking at lots. I haven't found one yet, but I'll recognize it when I see it. I haven't found it in Russellville; I might have to look in Little Rock.

Kevin will build it for me. I've started looking at house plans. I know basically what I want and have started to work on the details. I'm excited about it, but I won't start it until it can be my number-one project. My granddaughter Rebecca already has her order in for a ladder that slides along some bookshelves.

Jessica and Chuck were recently married in a small ceremony with close friends and family. This is a new beginning for her. Katherine and her family have moved from Russellville to Atlanta, where they have bought a lot and will build a new house. They are excited about their future. They'll be near Tallahassee, where Jonna and Scot now live with the newest addition to our family. John Thomas Patterson was born Thanksgiving Day, 1996.

Epilogue

——•——

Barry:
*There's a point where
everything becomes normal.*

Finding financial freedom

Sometimes when I drive to Hot Springs, I stop by the grave of my first client, Carroll Plumlee. I will never forget him. Sometimes I have a little conversation with him: *You wanted to make sure Gloria would be OK. Carroll, she's OK. She's going to have enough.*

Gloria will never forget Carroll, either. I'd be surprised if she goes a day without thinking about him, even after having lived without him for more than fifteen years. But she very much has her own life. She loves opera; she's involved with her church; she travels occasionally to Europe and takes a relative.

There are very specific things about her life that are different from the life she led with Carroll. Her house is hers. She made the decision about how it was going to be shaped, how far down the hill it was going to be built, the colors, the landscaping.

After many years, Gloria is far beyond what Carroll and I could have imagined back then. There is nothing in her portfolio with Carroll's fingerprints still on it. All of the investments are hers. She understands and manages her own financial matters.

Sharon now shares a business with someone else. This is not necessarily a bad thing, but it's awkward and confusing. At some point that company will be sold and Sharon will do something with that money: she'll convert it to stocks or bonds or maybe another business. But that will be the result of *her* work, *her* learning, *her* understanding, *her* decisions. No one is going to forget John or what John created, but before long, Sharon's attitude toward her finances — like her attitudes about many facets of her life — will be very different. She is learning how to manage her financial matters. Everything will one day be based on decisions *she* has made.

Advisors who chose to work with her as "John Trusty's widow" instead of Sharon Trusty made an error in their professional relationships with her. She's not going to remain the same. When she started breaking old ties with some of the people who didn't want the old ties to be broken, she started going forward. It's been very, very difficult for her to do that. I have laid out the scope of the work that lies ahead; there is much work yet to do, much to understand and learn.

Sharon has faced some very difficult issues. But she is really moving forward with confidence. In the financial world, a thoughtful and informed analysis of facts will generally lead you to a wise conclusion. It's easy for me to analyze and explain information. But it is far more difficult and challenging for her to decide and accept.

No widow with whom I have worked for longer than a few years lacks confidence and security. Each one has come to accept her situation and has dealt with her emotions. Each has dealt with them in her own particular, private way. But it is so evident: over a period of time each one has come to have confidence, has become aware she is financially capable. Each understands that the quantity of capital she has will provide her standard of living for the rest of her life.

Each widow has come to this point from a profound sense of insecurity — even if she had a lot of assets. It doesn't make any difference how many times she has seen the numbers or the reports, each one takes in that information only in her own time. In *every* case it has taken many months, even years. But at some point each widow has realized she has a reliable, new decision partner. The decision partner doesn't replace her husband; but each one comes to have confidence that she is working with a competent and reliable person. From the experience of making lots of decisions and seeing the fruits of those decisions, her confidence grows.

Sharon is definitely headed in the direction of that kind of confidence, of dealing with her financial situation head-on. Eventually she will have no fear of her financial circumstances. Her life will be occupied with other things. She will be involved in planning a trip, shopping for Christmas gifts, doing volunteer work, writing another book, working in politics—or building her own business—things that a woman, a mother, a grandmother, a friend does. She will be free of the past. What she has will be hers. When she gets to that point, she will have financial freedom.

I can objectively see what work can be done here and should be done there. Certainly I learn with every client, but working with Sharon has taught me an unusual amount. When I think about working with widows there comes a time when I see that they are so different—so very different—from the way they used to be. When we have a meeting and I ask if everything is OK, I can see the difference. I have that tremendous satisfaction that this person's life is going well and that I had something to do with it.

I know that part of this change is their acceptance of their circumstances. They have control over their financial lives and the fear is gone. Whether they remarry, whether they are dating, whether they are making investment decisions, there is a point where everything becomes normal, where everything that wasn't going right starts to flow.

Additional Resources

- Charles A. Jaffe, *The Right Way to Hire Financial Help* (Cambridge: MIT Press, 1998).
- "Questions to Ask When Choosing a Financial Planner," Consumer Information Center, Dept. 22, Pueblo, CO 81009
- National Association of Personal Financial Advisors: 888-333-6659; www.napfa.org
- Certified Financial Planner Board of Standards:* 888-237-6275; www.CFP-Board.org
- American Institute of Certified Public Accountants: www.aicpa.org
- North American Securities Administrators Assoc.: 888-846-2722; www.nasaa.org
- National Association of Insurance Commissioners: 816-842-3600; www.naic.org
- National Association of Securities Dealers: 800-289-9999; www.nasdr.com
- American Bar Association: www.abanet.org
- National Academy of Elder Law Attorneys: www.naela.org
- Securities and Exchange Commission: 800-732-0330; www.sec.gov
- Social Security: 800-772-1213; www.ssa.gov

* As we go to press, members of the INTERNATIONAL ASSOCIATION OF FINANCIAL PLANNING and the INSTITUTE OF CERTIFIED FINANCIAL PLANNERS are voting on a merger of the two organizations. If the motion passes, the new organization name will be FINANCIAL PLANNING ASSOCIATION.

- David Burns, *The Feeling Good Handbook* (New York: Plume, 1999).

- American Association of Retired Persons:
  601 E Street, NW, Washington, DC 20049; 202-434-2277.
  The AARP Grief and Loss Program has a great deal of online information on coping with grief and loss at:
  www.aarp.org/griefandloss

- THEOS for the Widowed, a non-profit organization for the widowed, with chapters and support groups all over the US:
  1301 Clark Building, 717 Liberty Ave., Pittsburgh, PA 15222;
  412-471-7779

- *Bereavement Magazine*, published every two months:
  Bereavement Publishing, Inc., 5125 North Union Blvd., Ste #4,
  Colorado Springs, CO 80918; 719-266-0006;
  e-mail: grief@usa.net

- *Thanatos*, a realistic journal concerning dying, death and bereavement:
  Florida Funeral Directors Service, Inc., P.O. Box 6009,
  Tallahassee, FL 32314; 904-224-1969

Appendix 1

Social Security

Survivor benefits provided through Social Security can be very important; unfortunately, the Social Security laws are very complex and often misunderstood. Widows are often surprised to discover the reality of their benefits. For instance, a widow under the age of sixty-two receives no survivor benefits unless she has children under age nineteen in the household. Social Security pays a family benefit for children, but after they turn eighteen, the benefits stop. A widow is not eligible for benefits again until she reaches the normal retirement age.

Depending on your year of birth, your normal retirement age will be age sixty-five or greater. Anyone, however, can take a reduced retirement benefit at age sixty-two, and widows may be eligible for a reduced retirement benefit at age sixty.

The amount of the widow benefit is determined by the wages earned by her or her husband. If both husband and wife have taxable wages, the benefit is based on the greater of the two.

It is a good idea to check on the status of your account. The Social Security Administration has a toll-free telephone number (1–800–772–1213) you can call to obtain the form necessary to request the information on your account. Within a few weeks after submitting this form, you will receive a detailed packet of information called "Personal Earnings and Benefits Estimate Statement." This statement includes your normal and early retirement benefits, delayed retirement benefits, and benefits payable to a surviving spouse and dependent children.

Appendix 2

Debt

Many of us have the attitude that the best debt is no debt. We have heard stories of families losing their homes or businesses because of debt. During the 1980s, many farmers sold their family farms at auction because of debt. The news surrounding this was often sensational—some farmers even committed suicide. Losing your home or business at auction or through repossession is an emotional nightmare. The idea that it could happen to us cultivates a fear of debt.

You must answer two questions before you increase your debt. First, "Is this idea financially sound?" Let's say that you have inherited a modest amount from a distant aunt and your spouse wants to reduce or pay off your home mortgage. Should you or shouldn't you? Here is the analysis:

> If the rate on your mortgage is 9% and you are in a 35% tax bracket, the after-tax "cost" of borrowing that money is approximately 6% ([9% x .35 = 3%] then [9% - 3% = 6%]). If you can buy a 6% municipal bond or stocks, that grow more than 8 to 10%, you should invest the inheritance and keep making the mortgage payments. At the end of the mortgage your investment will have grown.

What if you pay off the mortgage and start saving an amount equal to the old mortgage payment? This strategy rarely works. First you have to be very disciplined to save that monthly amount when the mortgage company is not breathing down your neck. Second, if you project the numbers, you will discover less money has accumulated at the end. Finally, we all know that as a debt gets older more of the payment is principal and less of it is interest. Many times you are simply not saving much by paying off an older loan.

Another issue is what you do with the resulting cash flow. If you spend the inheritance on a lavish Caribbean cruise or that new sports car, are you meeting your financial needs? If the objective is to accumulate wealth, having debt may be a logical conclusion.

The other question we should ask ourselves is "How much debt should I have?" It is the amount of debt we incur that is the source of all those horror stories. You see not all American farmers lost their farms—only those who have *excessive* debt. We should have only the amount of debt that we can comfortably afford. There is no set rule for the amount of debt we should have. The proper amount depends on earning power, the amount of assets, age, and other factors.

Most importantly, don't depend on banks or financial institutions to keep you within the reasonable amount of debt. Debt is unfortunately too easy to get these days. Remember that lenders profit from your loan, so they *want* you to borrow money. It is best to seek other opinions about decisions relating to more debt.

Having debt is not necessarily a bad thing; *excessive* debt is. What we do with the money from the loan determines whether it makes sense to borrow money.